Eyes That See Not

Eyes That See Not

The Pope Looks at Jesus

Gerd Lüdemann

Assisted by Tom Hall

POLEBRIDGE PRESS
Santa Rosa, California

Beliefs are not necessarily facts
To Marei Lüdemann & David Perrin
on their wedding August 19, 2007

Copyright © 2008 by Gerd Lüdemann

All rights reserved. Printed in the United States of America. No part of this book may be used or reproduced in any manner whatsoever without written permission except in the case of brief quotations embodied in critical articles and reviews. For information address Polebridge Press, P. O. Box 7268, Santa Rosa, California 95407.

Cover and interior design by Robaire Ream

Library of Congress Cataloging-in-Publication Data
Lüdemann, Gerd.
  [Jesusbild des Papstes. English]
  Eyes that see not : the Pope looks at Jesus / Gerd Lüdemann.
     p. cm.
  Includes bibliographical references and index.
  ISBN-13: 978-1-59815-006-3 (alk. paper)
  1. Benedict XVI, Pope, 1927- Jesus von Nazareth. 2. Jesus Christ--Biography. 3. Bible. N.T. Gospels--Criticism, interpretation, etc. I. Title.
  BT301.9.L8313 2008
  232.9'01--dc22
                                                              2007052284

Contents

Preface	vii
Prologue	ix

Overview and Critique

Chapter One on the Foreword	3
Chapter Two on the Introduction: An Initial Reflection . . .	13
Chapter Three on Chap. 1: The Baptism of Jesus	17
Chapter Four on Chap. 2: The Temptations of Jesus	23
Chapter Five on Chap. 3: . . . the Kingdom of God	33
Chapter Six on Chap. 4: The Sermon on the Mount	43
Chapter Seven on Chap. 5: The Lord's Prayer	57
Chapter Eight on Chap. 6: The Disciples	63
Chapter Nine on Chap. 7: The Message of the Parables	69
Chapter Ten on Chap. 8: . . . John's Gospel	79
Chapter Eleven on Chap. 9: Peter's Confession . . .	99
Chapter Twelve on Chap. 10: Jesus Declares His Identity	109
Epilogue: Ten Objections to Joseph Ratzinger's Book on Jesus	119
Notes	122
Works Consulted	128
Index	130

Preface

It is an unfortunate observation that today's society is amply supplied with uninformed persons who raise their voices on all kinds of issues. Consequently, public discussion is often marred by a lack of knowledge—perhaps most notably when the subject at hand is religion or Church.

For centuries, of course, Universities have been bastions of the free inquiry and unfettered research that are part and parcel of the scientific method. Indeed, the resulting advances in both science and the humanities have led to a flowering in all aspects of human life, including religion and Church. And because of their commitment to objectivity, the Universities have been bulwarks against superstition of every sort. Therefore, when the Pope—the leader and chief spokesman of more than a billion Catholics—publishes a book that purports to study the life of Jesus of Nazareth, it is both reasonable and requisite for representatives of academic theology to examine it and to review its objective value. With that in mind, I herewith present the results of my assessment. Beginning with a brief overview of my findings, I proceed to a point-by-point examination of the papal exposition and close with a reiteration of basic points and problems raised. It may in fact be of help to read the Epilogue first as a brief introduction to the main argument of the book.

Unless otherwise indicated the translations of the New Testament texts are my own.

My heartfelt thanks go to Martha Cunningham for offering generous criticism and to Tom Hall for his great care in making my English more readable. The present version of the book owes a great deal to his kind sharing of ideas and formulating of conclusions.

Gerd Lüdemann
Theological Faculty
Georg-August-University Göttingen, Germany
Website: gerdluedemann.de

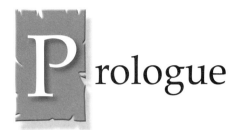
Prologue

In his insightful book *The Historian and the Believer,* Van Harvey drives home the point that history must be carefully distinguished from belief and identifies the crucial difference between the two: the historian is obliged to present objective evidence for his assertions. The rules of the game do not permit him to rely on uncorroborated testimony or claims of authority. Thus the validity of the historian's conclusions derives from the very nature of historical knowledge. The chronicler who fails to challenge eyewitness testimony and to submit documentary sources to critical examination is not an historian. Rather he or she becomes, in Harvey's trenchant but apt words, "no longer a seeker of knowledge but a mediator of past belief; not a thinker but a transmitter of tradition."[1]

However undeniable, indeed axiomatic, the truth of Van Harvey's observation may seem, the flood of ill-informed publications about Jesus continues to rise despite the efforts of a number of both Protestant and Catholic scholars who continue to make lasting contributions to our understanding of the New Testament. Yes, for some time now Catholic scholarship has been notably driven by the historical-critical impulse and has produced major commentaries and analytical works.

Even Joseph Ratzinger, in his recently published first volume of a book on Jesus,[2] praises historical method in the highest terms and lays great stress on its necessity (xv). The Christian faith, he avows, is based on and undergirded by the Bible's essentially authentic reflection of actual historical events, and as such is to be strictly distinguished from dispensations based on ancient myths (xv).

And yet in virtually the same breath we are warned that when applied to the Scriptures, the historical method has limits that must be recognized and respected. The rules governing critical research, Benedict insists, have restricted applicability in the case of the Bible, inasmuch as the text is divinely inspired and intended for the instruction of the Church. The historical-critical method "does not exhaust the interpretative task for someone who sees the biblical writings as a single corpus of Holy Scripture inspired by God" (xvi). He proposes, for example, that only through faith can one discern the profound harmony underlying the New Testament portraits of Jesus. Indeed, he sees faith-based restrictions on the work of historians to be not only consonant with historical reason but its very basis, and therefore entirely consistent with the historical nature of the individual biblical texts (xix).

Benedict makes it plain at the very outset that a primary motive of his book is to eliminate a conceptual disconnect that he says began to arise in the 1950s—the gap between the historical Jesus and the Christ of faith (xi). It comes as no surprise, then, that in summarizing his remarks on methodology, he grounds his portrayal of Jesus on his trust in the truth of the New Testament gospels (xxi). What he gave with one hand, he quickly withdrew with the other.

The problem is that while Benedict implicitly grants the scholarly consensus that the gospel portraits of Jesus are artistic compositions, he seems to ignore the fact that some of their dissimilarities amount to mutual contradiction! To put the case bluntly, his statements of purpose and method not only repudiate the approaches and results of the last 250 years of biblical criticism, but also resemble—no doubt unintentionally—the recent flood of popular writings about Jesus. To be sure, this time it is not hidden documents in the Vatican or rediscovered ossuaries of Jesus and his relatives that underlie the argument, but we find the equally dubious thesis of the inherent factual reliability of the gospels. On that basis, of course, speculative assertions supporting the unity of the historical Jesus and the Christ of faith can multiply freely. But that approach ignores a vital preliminary: an objective examination of the value of the gospels. In short it begs the question.

Like the Church Fathers before him Ratzinger uses meditations cast in historical form to translate and project the so-called revelatory event of Christ into the present. At the same time these meditations point to the eucharistic aspect of Jesus' life and thus proclaim its sacramental purpose. Thus Ratzinger's book is infused with and inseparable from a mystery that only faith can understand. To any who cannot accept his supernatural claims and postulates, it must remain either an enigma or an absurdity. Unless, of course, one were to embrace the supernatural view of things and submit to God's call for repentance.

But we do not live in antiquity, or even in the Middle Ages. In our world metaphysical or meta-historical statements do not go without saying, but may need to be argued anew. Science and the arts have long been autonomous, radically independent of doctrinal belief.

That epitomizes the nature of the revolution that, beginning with the Enlightenment, has shaped the modern world. One element of that intellectual and perceptual revolution has been the non-metaphysical analysis of the New Testament gospels, an enterprise of more than two centuries given over to examining their sources, their textual histories, the purposes of their authors, and the historical reliability of their accounts. Even a superficial acquaintance with the results of this quest reveals that Ratzinger's Jesus book fails to match historical reality. The recoil from his attack on historical critics for having a too narrow understanding of reality sends his shot wide of the mark: lacking any solid commitment to empirical truth, he confuses the historical Jesus with his imagined heavenly Lord. In spite of repeated apologetic exhortations, he fails to merge the heavenly savior of souls and the human teacher of righteousness in a unified portrait. His bold but ultimately manipulative handling of the New Testament sources would fail to pass muster before any board of academic historians or any forum of independent theologians. His truth claims have no context of credibility beyond the hermetic confines of a carefully controlled world of faith.

In a desperate effort to defend both the historicity of the canonical Jesus and his function as the revealer of God, Ratzinger invokes the existence of two different orders of reality: the temporal or earthly reality that appears in history, and the eternal or heavenly reality that is available only to faith through revelation. In this respect he is in harmony with the fathers of the ancient Church who applied physical and metaphysical, historical and meta-historical categories to the "revelation of God in Jesus Christ."

Ratzinger's description of this "event" as something outside the normal course of history corresponds to his understanding of the Bible: having a nature of its own, revelation generates a sacred history that is not sullied by the world. (In other words, it is entirely special pleading.) And, unique among literary forms, Holy Scripture is self-attesting. Accordingly, a specific image of Jesus permeates Ratzinger's book: that of the Son who has the same nature as God, who is fully divine and at the same time fully human. Apparently unimpressed by the obvious historical incongruity, Ratzinger describes Jesus as God come down to earth, having emptied himself on behalf of sinful human beings and promising to lead those who believe in him into his heavenly kingdom. Having brought this image of Jesus to his reading of the text, he then rediscovers it in the four gospels. He impugns historical critics for sharing a one-sided understanding of reality. Against their approach he claims to know that Jesus, the "Son" was already with the Father before the creation. Moreover, in God himself an eternal dialogue takes place between Father and Son—who together with the Holy Spirit comprise one and the same God. For Ratzinger this is not a myth but a statement of the supreme cosmic reality, and the corresponding texts are to be understood literally.

But such subjective notions of reality can have no place in the academy, and in fact find little serious support in the world at large. A growing number of Christians find such mythic definitions of what William James called "the unseen order of things" to be both patronizing and inept.

A detailed answer to Ratzinger's Jesus book is necessary for two more reasons. First, the enthusiastic response it has received even among educated people reflects the fact that the very existence of biblical criticism is widely unknown. Second, many Catholic biblical scholars will be understandably intimidated by the prospect of essaying an honest evaluation of the Pope's pronouncements. Accordingly, I have undertaken the task of defending historical reason and exposing the fallacies of his self-serving interpretation of the Bible.

Since Ratzinger bases his arguments mainly on biblical passages, my dialogue with his book will consist largely of exegeses of "Holy Scripture"—that is to say I shall deal with the texts by employing the very historical-critical approach that he claims to follow. Thereby I hope to open a constructive debate on how reasonable twenty-first century people should read the Bible. To that end, I shall attempt to provide clear and intellectually defensible insights into a collection of ancient writings from now-alien cultures, and thus enable the reader to form a better understanding of the Bible as a whole and Jesus of Nazareth in particular.

In effect, I am offering what I hope will prove an irresistible invitation: Rather than be a passive inheritor of an ancient and jealously mediated tradition, join me and thousands of independent seekers of knowledge, and become a thinker in your own right.

Overview and Critique

Chapter One

on the Foreword

Ratzinger's presupposition that the gospels present accurate historical accounts is wrongheaded.

Overview

At the very outset Ratzinger tells the reader that his book "has had a long gestation" (xi), during which he had become acquainted with two quite different approaches to Jesus. First, he was exposed to scholars[1] who based their view of the historical Jesus on the New Testament gospels. "They presented him as a man living on earth who, fully human though he was, at the same time brought God to men, the God with whom as Son he was one. Through the man Jesus, then, God was made visible, and hence our eyes were able to behold the perfect man" (xi). Then, since the early fifties of the last century, he encountered historical critics who distinguished between the Jesus of history and the Christ of faith, and actually discredited the historical value of the Gospels. Such an approach, he says, provoked a fundamental question: "[W]hat can faith in Jesus as the Christ possibly mean, in Jesus as the Son of the living God, if the *man* Jesus was so completely different from the picture that the Evangelists painted of him and that the Church, on the evidence of the Gospels, takes as the basis of her preaching?" (xi). Indeed, historical criticism led to "the impression that we have very little certain knowledge of Jesus and that only at a later stage did faith in his divinity shape the image we have of him" (xii). Such a situation is dramatic "for faith, because its point of reference is being placed in doubt" (xii).

Ratzinger illustrates the difficulty this poses for the Christian faith by referring to the noted Catholic exegete Rudolf Schnackenburg, in whose portrayal of Jesus an ambiguity persists. It is caused by the constraints of the historical-critical method, which despite its limitations Schnackenburg felt obliged to use. The result was that "a reliable view of the historical figure of Jesus of Nazareth through scientific effort with historical-critical methods can be only inadequately achieved."[2] Yet such statements do not clarify how solid the historical ground for the real Jesus is, and Ratzinger strives to go beyond Schnackenburg in this matter. In order to do so he uses as an historical vantage point Jesus' "communion with the Father, which is the true center of his personality; without it, we cannot understand him at all, and it is from this center that he makes himself present to us still today" (xiv).

Ratzinger then goes on to sketch the methodology—including his reliance on the doctrine of the divine inspiration of the biblical texts—that has guided him in writing this book. Since biblical faith is based on actual historical events, he grants, "the historical-critical method ... is and remains an indispensable dimension of exegetical work" (xv). By saying *et incarnatus est*,[3] he argues, "we acknowledge God's actual entry into real history" (xv).

But in three respects, he insists, the historical-critical method has limitations:

1. "For someone who considers himself directly addressed by the Bible today, the method's first limit is that by its very nature it has to leave the biblical word in the past" (xvi).
2. "Because it is a historical method, it presupposes the uniformity of the context within which the events of history unfold. It must therefore treat the biblical word it investigates as human words" (xvi–xvii).
3. "The unity of all of these writings as one 'Bible' ... is not something it can recognize as an immediate historical datum" (xvii).

Yet according to Ratzinger the historical-critical method points beyond itself "and contains within itself an openness to complementary methods. In these words from the past, we can discern the question concerning their meaning for today; a voice greater than man's echoes in Scripture's human words; the individual writings ... of the Bible point somehow to the living process that shapes the one Scripture" (xviii).

The latter point has been emphasized by the so-called "canonical exegesis"[4] a project developed in the last decades in North America whose aim is "to read individual texts within the totality of the one Scripture, which then sheds new light on all the individual texts" (xviii). It is hardly surprising that in spite of the fragmented nature of the scriptural data, Christ turns out to be the center of Scripture and the unity of both testaments is established. "This process is certainly not linear, and it is often dramatic, but when you watch it unfold in light of Jesus Christ, you can see it moving in a single overall direction; you can see that the Old and the New Testament belong together" (xix). Admittedly, this Christological—indeed christo*centric*—reading that confers unity on the Bible necessarily presumes faith, and therefore "cannot be the conclusion of a purely historical method. But this act of faith is based upon reason—historical reason—and so makes it possible to see the internal unity of Scripture" (xix). Moreover, he assures us that it does not deprive the individual texts of Scripture of their originality.[5] Canonical exegesis is thus "an essential dimension of exegesis. It does not contradict historical-critical interpretation, but carries it forward in an organic way toward becoming theology in the proper sense" (xix).

Two additional aspects of theological exegesis should, we are told, be taken into account. First, although historical-critical interpretation tries to establish the original intention of a specific text at a given situation, every human word of some weight carries a "deeper value" within itself than its author is aware of. "This 'deeper value' pertains most of all to words that have matured in the course of faith-history" (xx).

Second, neither "the individual books of Holy Scripture nor the Scripture as a whole are simply a piece of literature. The Scripture emerged from within the heart of a living subject—the pilgrim People of God—and lives within this same subject" (xx). The necessary conclusion of this is clear: "The People of God—the Church—is the living subject of Scripture; it is in the Church that the words of the Bible are always in the present. This also means, of course, that the People has to receive its very self from God, ultimately from the incarnate Christ; it has to let itself be ordered, guided, and led by him" (xxi).

Ratzinger is fully aware that his discourse on the proper method of interpreting Scripture has an important consequence for his attempt to understand the central figure of the New Testament:

> The main implication of this for my portrayal of Jesus is that I trust the Gospels. Of course, I take for granted everything that the Council and modern exegesis tell us about literary genres, about authorial intention, and about the fact that the Gospels were written in the context, and speak within the living milieu, of communities. I have tried, to the best of my ability, to incorporate all of this, and yet I wanted to try to portray the Jesus of the Gospels as the real, "historical" Jesus in the strict sense of the word. (xxi–xxii)

In other words, this "Jesus of the gospels"—who in the two previous paragraphs was described as a product of the self-transcendent People of God, the Church that in turn received "its very self from the incarnate Christ"—is now to be portrayed as "real," "plausible," and "convincing" using the historical-critical method! The ontological disconnect leaves one breathless.

Modern research has carefully examined the rise of Christology during the first two decades after Jesus' death, and has ascribed it to anonymous collective formulations. Yet to Ratzinger it seems to be more reasonable "to assume that the greatness came at the beginning" (xxii). At the same time, he concedes, "to believe that, as man, he truly *was* God, and that he communicated his divinity veiled in parables, yet with increasing clarity, exceeds the scope of the historical method" (xxiii). Is there a way out of this dire impasse? Of course! If "we take this conviction of faith as our starting point for reading the texts with the help of historical methodology and its intrinsic openness to something greater, they are opened up and they reveal a way and a figure that are worthy of belief" (xxiii).

Ratzinger is aware that much of what he says goes beyond the historical-critical method; to describe it as intrinsically open to something greater is at best disingenuous. Indeed, his stated purpose is to counter modern exegesis—even though he claims "profound gratitude for all that it has given and continues to give to us" (xxiii). In the last analysis, however, he seeks "to go beyond purely historical-critical exegesis so as to apply new methodological insights that allow us to offer a properly theological interpretation of the Bible. To be sure, this requires faith, but the aim unequivocally is not, nor should be, to give up serious engagement with history" (xxiii). In fact, this is precisely what it does—it jettisons the critical method and any contact with history. In short, it is a refusal to see the implications of living in time.

Critique

On pp. xiv–xvi: In presupposing the divine inspiration of Scripture Ratzinger employs a dogmatic method of biblical interpretation. If at the outset exegesis does not strive to discover from the text what its author wanted to say, what it meant at a given time, then arbitrariness of interpretation has already begun. Why bother to interpret an ancient text using rational criteria if ecclesiastical rather than scientific standards guide us from the start?

More than a century ago the German theologian Ernst Troeltsch described the dogmatic method and thereby contributed to its decline and eventual abandonment by honest, critical thinkers:

> Its nature is that it possesses whatever authority it has precisely *because* it reaches beyond the kind of historical developments that are analogous to other historical happenings, and therefore it stands beyond the reach of historical criticism. Although it claims to be based on history, it is not itself history of the normal, secular sort, not like critical history writing. Rather, it is salvation-history: connected data presenting the promise of salvation, and employing "facts" that are visible and convincing only to believers. Indeed, these "facts" do not have the characteristics that critical history writing requires of its data.[6]

This is, of course, precisely Ratzinger's method: he offers lip-service to historical criticism, but quickly discards it in order to elevate totally speculative concepts and doctrines to the level of absolute truth. In fact, we should understand as a firm caveat his opening pledge to apply both historical criticism and the doctrine of Jesus' divine Sonship to the business of showing that the Jesus of history and the Christ of faith are one and the same person. This statement demonstrates beyond cavil that he has unalterably decided the issue of the historical-critical method: it is a bothersome bit of modernism that is to be repudiated whenever it gets in the way of doctrinal or kerygmatic concerns

On p. xxi: In view of the generally accepted history of the formation of the gospels, Ratzinger's claim to trust their historical accuracy cannot be accepted. The following facts must be taken into account:

1. Trusting the gospels and reading them as supplementing one another is an anachronism in view of modern scholarship's adoption of the Two Documents Hypothesis, which clearly disallows such an approach. According to this hypothesis Matthew and Luke used both Mark and the Sayings Gospel Q (from the German "Quelle", meaning "source") and did so independently of one another, but eyewitnesses composed none of these.

2. John is the latest gospel and is equally devoid of eyewitness testimony.[7]

3. From Luke's preface to his gospel (Luke 1:1–4)[8] we gain important information about the rise and transmission of the earliest reports about Jesus—information that helps us to form balanced judgments about the historical value of the gospels.

> *Luke 1:1–4*
> [1]Since many have attempted to compose a narrative about the events which have come to fulfillment among us, [2]as they have been handed down to us from those who from the beginning were themselves eyewitnesses and servants of the word, [3]I too have thought it good, since I have investigated everything carefully from the start, to write them out in order for you, excellent Theophilus, [4]in order that you know the certain basis of the teaching in which you have been instructed.

This magnificently stylized sentence—translated by me, with intentional adherence to Greek syntactic form—is without parallel in the New Testament. The only passage in the Synoptic Gospels in which an evangelist gives explicit information about the aim of his work and his sources, it emphasizes the author's literary dependence and thus provides us with important insights. *First,* a number of others (*polloi* = "many") had written gospels before Luke (v 1). *Second,* these writers were no more present at the events they describe than Luke was. The only one so qualified are the group of "eyewitnesses and servants of the word" who are the sources of the tradition (v 2). *Third,* Luke wants to surpass his predecessors (indeed, the verb "attempt" connotes his critique of the quality of their works), since he has investigated all the existing accounts so as to write things down in the proper order (v 3). In the course of his work he has in many cases corrected his sources—and that means both Mark and Q—and various traditions passed down by the servants of the word. *Fourth,* according to Luke his work is intended to serve as a foundation for faith; in other words, only this correct account can be the basis of Christian doctrine (v 4). In short, faith must be grounded in verifiable historical realities; hearsay and opinion are not to be considered dependable in such a crucial matter.

This passage is vital for judging the question of the origin of the Jesus traditions. What emerges from it is this: First came the oral tradition of the eyewitnesses and servants of the word, none of whom set down his recollections about Jesus in writing. That happened only later, and certainly more than one or two gospels came into being in this way. But these several written accounts had not yet gained significant and widespread respect. Therefore, based on his knowledge of Mark, Q, and several other sources, Luke intends to supersede—and probably replace—these earlier works with his gospel.

4. The narratives of the New Testament gospels contradict one another at many places. Let me point to Jesus' words on the cross as noteworthy examples. I shall offer short comments thus clarifying their historical value.

Mark 15:34
At the ninth hour Jesus cried out with a loud voice, "*Elohi, Elohi, lama sabachthani?*" which means, "My God, my God, why have you forsaken me?"

Jesus' cry of despair corresponds word for word with Psalm 22:2—with the exception that there God is addressed in Hebrew as *Eli,* whereas Mark has the Aramaic *Elohi.* Although Jesus spoke Aramaic, the very fact that Mark used the Aramaic equivalent is an argument against its historicity. It would have been impossible (as is reported in the subsequent verse) for Roman soldiers to have heard the words *Elohi,* etc., uttered in Aramaic, as a prayer to Elijah: "And some of the bystanders hearing it said, 'Look, he is calling Elijah'."

And we cannot imagine witnesses other than the soldiers, since the women are said to have observed Jesus' death on the cross only from a distance (Mark 15:40–41)—and one may reasonably doubt whether this note has any historical value. Finally, two other reasons tell against the historicity of this cry of Jesus from the cross. *First,* as we shall see below, contradictory reports of Jesus' words from the cross were handed down.

Second, this passage reflects the primitive Christians' need to create a crucifixion scene with borrowings from the Old Testament. For not only did they lack eyewitness information, but liturgical concerns were at work (note that Psalms 22, 31, and 69 provided most of the material): it was edifying to read the passion story in the light of the Psalter, for that helped to soften the unpalatable recollection that God's Son, who was daily present in worship, had had to drink the bitter cup of death.

Matthew 27:46b
About the ninth hour Jesus cried with a loud voice, "*Eli, Eli, lama sabachthani,*" that is, "My God, my God, why have you forsaken me?"

Matthew presupposes Mark 15:34 but changes "Elohi" to the Hebrew "Eli." In so doing he is following Psalm 22:2 and explaining how the Roman soldiers might have understood Jesus' cry as addressed to Elijah. The historicity of this passage can be ruled out because Matthew was not an eyewitness, but was simply appropriating Mark 15:34.

Luke 23:34a
Father, forgive them; for they do not know what they are doing.

The Lukan account of the crucifixion has no recognized sources other than the Gospel of Mark. This means that any divergence from the Markan report must be regarded as an addition by Luke. Consequently, not only all three sayings he attributes to Jesus on the cross (Luke 23:34a, 43b, and 46b) derive from his pen, but also Mark 15:34 has been purposely omitted.

Also of interest is the fact that Luke 23:34a is lacking in a number of important ancient manuscripts. If it represents a received but little-known tradition (and not a later scribal insertion), perhaps "Luke" placed it here to create a parallel with the prayer he assigned to the first Christian martyr, Stephen, in Acts 7:60: "Lord, do not hold this sin against them!"

Luke 23:43b
Truly, I say to you, today you will be with me in paradise.

This verse gives Jesus' reply to the request of one of the two men who were reportedly crucified with him (v 42: "Jesus, remember me when you come into your kingdom") and additionally presupposes his ascent from the cross. The saying seems to represent an attempt to rationalize the delay of the Second Coming: Jesus' disciples will not attain heaven only at the end of the age, as was the earliest Christian expectation, but immediately after death. That Luke might not have cared about the contradiction between the ascent of Jesus from the cross and his ascension late on Easter Day (Luke 24:51) is evident from his report in Acts 1:9 of yet another ascension forty days later. And, of course, if the saying is in any way related to the delay of the Second Coming, it cannot possibly be historical.

Luke 23:46b
Father, into your hands I commend my spirit.

This speech corresponds to Ps 31:6 and derives from the aforementioned early Christian tendency to interpret the passion of Jesus in the light of Old Testament psalms.

John 19:25–27
[25]Now standing by the cross of Jesus were his mother, and his mother's sister, Mary the wife of Clopas, and Mary Magdalene. [26]When Jesus saw his mother and the disciple whom he loved standing near, he said to his mother, "Woman, behold, your son!" [27]Then he said to the disciple, "Behold, your mother!" And from that hour the disciple took her into his own home.

In view of the precise enumeration of the women in v 25, a list that surprisingly includes the mother of Jesus (who is not placed in this scene by the other three New Testament Gospels), it is striking that according to vv 26–27 the Beloved Disciple, previously unmentioned, was standing with them by the cross. It indicates that here John has dramatized a piece of tradition that reported a bond between Mary and the Beloved Disciple by connecting it with Jesus' last hours; it also shows that the report originally had nothing to do with the death of Jesus.

The scene cannot be historical, for in Mark 15:40–41 (Matt 27:55; Luke 23:49) the women observe *from afar* what is happening on the cross, and neither Jesus' mother nor a disciple appears with the women who observe the crucifixion.

John 19:30
It is finished.

According to the Fourth Gospel's theological concept, the passion of Jesus is the completion of the mission of the Son of God. Through his death on the cross he returns to the glory that he had from the very beginning as the Pre-existent One (cf. John 1). John can even say that the crucifixion of Jesus is identical with his exaltation to the Father (cf. 3:14; 8:28) or his glorification (cf. 12:23, 28; 13:31–32; 17:1, 5). It is in keeping with this that even on the cross Jesus remains the Lord: still in command, unbroken, and unshaken. For this reason the evangelist omits any cry of despair, and instead assigns to Jesus the triumphant saying, "It is finished." This speech, then, derives exclusively from the Fourth Gospel's high Christology, and is therefore clearly inauthentic.

THE BOTTOM LINE: Ratzinger's ideological commitment to the fundamental accuracy of the gospel record, while perhaps theologically understandable, is intellectually dishonest; it puts him in the position of barking up the wrong tree and points his work in the wrong direction.

Chapter Two
on the Introduction
An Initial Reflection on the Mystery of Jesus

Ratzinger pretends to embrace the historical method while holding it at arm's length.

Overview

In this section Ratzinger begins his reflections with a look at the promise of Moses (Deut 18:15) that "your God will raise up for you a prophet like me from among you" (2–3). Yet a strange melancholy hangs over the ending of the fifth Book of Moses, he says, for that promise remained unfulfilled. And even Moses' relation to God was limited, since although he conversed with God, he did not behold God's face (5). Therefore, the "promise of a 'prophet like me' . . . implicitly contains an even greater expectation: that the last prophet, the new Moses, will be granted what was refused to the first one—a real, immediate vision of the face of God, and thus the ability to speak entirely from seeing [sic], not just from looking at God's back" (5–6).

Ratzinger then points to John 1:18[1] as evidence that in Jesus "the promise of the new prophet is fulfilled. What was true of Moses only in fragmentary form has now been fully realized in the person of Jesus: He lives before the face of God, not just as a friend, but as a Son; he lives in the most intimate unity with the Father" (6).

Benedict has no doubt that his interpretation is fundamental:

> We have to start here if we are truly to understand the figure of Jesus as it is presented to us in the New Testament; all that we are told about his words, deeds, sufferings, and glory is anchored here. This is the central point, and if we leave it out of account, we fail to grasp what the figure of Jesus is really all about, so that it becomes self-contradictory and, in the end, unintelligible. The question that every reader of the New Testament must ask—where Jesus' teaching came from, how his appearance in history is to be explained—can really be answered only from this perspective. (6)

Indeed, we are told, Jesus did not receive his teaching from human sources. Rather, it "originates from immediate contact with the Father, from 'face-to-face' dialogue—from the vision of the one who rests close to the Father's heart. It is the Son's words. Without this inner grounding, his teaching would be pure presumption. That is just what the learned men of Jesus' time judged it to be" (7).

What is more, Ratzinger emphasizes that the short passages in the gospels that tell of Jesus withdrawing "to the mountain" and spending nights in prayer "alone" are essential to our understanding of him, for "they lift the veil of mystery just a little; they give us a glimpse into Jesus' filial existence, into the source from which his action and teaching and suffering sprang" (7). Thus Ratzinger repudiates Adolf von Harnack's famous disavowal of Christology by vigorously denying the latter's assertion that "Jesus' message was about the Father, not about the Son, and that Christology therefore has no place in it" (7).[2] For Ratzinger, a high Christology is essential to understanding who Jesus really was: "the mystery of the Son as revealer of the Father . . . is present in everything Jesus says and does" (7).

Critique

On pp. 2–6: Ratzinger's arguments about Jesus' being the new Moses are not only speculative, but they rely on metaphors and analogies that have no place in a discourse on historical grounding. Thus they must be dismissed as irrelevant. Once again we see dogma infringing on scientific argument—belief, not fact, is Ratzinger's concern.

On p. 7: The statement that Jesus was divinely inspired and that his teaching therefore did not derive from human learning is absurd. Human beings do learn from one another, and certainly his father made him familiar with the basics of Jewish law. Concerning Ratzinger's claim that Jesus received a special revelation from God (with whom he is an equal), one is obliged to insist that so far he has not given one shred of real evidence for such an assertion—one that in any case can never find historical support because its avowed source is a mystery![3]

The brief reports about Jesus' withdrawing to a mountain and spending a night in solitary prayer can hardly be taken as historically sound, as he was, of course, devoid of witnesses. Even if he did as is reported, this has no bearing on the nature of any encounter with God. At least with Moses we hear of a physical event; from Jesus all we learn is that he goes away. His inclination toward prayer—more prevalent in Luke than in the other gospels, incidentally—is not unusual in spiritual persons. And the choice of a mountain, as in Deuteronomy, is common to metaphors about encounters with divine beings, who, among other things, were depicted as residing on high. The prayerful person who heads up the mountain depicts someone more likely to be close to God; but such a special relation is not factually verifiable.

THE BOTTOM LINE: In view of these purely dogmatic statements, inferred from "the mystery of the Son," the careful reader cannot help wondering how seriously to take Ratzinger's earlier commendation of the historical-critical method.[4]

Chapter Three

on Chapter 1

The Baptism of Jesus

Despite Ratzinger's pious protestations, the gospel record repudiates the claim that the doctrine of atonement has a basis in Jesus' baptism by John.

Overview

Ratzinger begins the chapter by noting that both Matthew and Luke give us evidence by which to date the beginning of the public ministry of Jesus (9–10). This turns what is at best a rhetorical turn of phrase into absolute fact, and is as unprovable as the consequent date of the "virgin birth." The one may follow from the other, but both are built on an historical house of cards. Moreover, and more to the point of our objection overall, Ratzinger proceeds, as usual, from the assertion of the factual to an apologetic for his reasoning—for, after all, "We are not meant to regard Jesus' activity as taking place in some sort of mythical 'anytime,' which can mean always or never. It is a precisely datable historical event having the full weight that real historical happenings have; like them, too, it happens once only; it is contemporary with all times, but not in the way that a timeless myth would be" (11).

After a summary overview of the political situation at the time of Jesus and the contemporary political parties—Zealots, Pharisees, Sadducees, and Essenes (12–14)—Ratzinger describes Jesus' baptism by John as a "concrete enactment of a conversion that gives the whole of life a new direction forever" (14)—an act that both proceeded from and demanded thenceforth "an ardent call to a new way of thinking and acting, but above all with the proclamation of God's judgment and with the announcement that one greater than John is to come" (14).

As to the curious and important relation of the Baptist to Jesus, Ratzinger explains, "The Fourth Gospel tells us that the Baptist 'did not know' (cf. Jn 1:30–33) this greater personage whose way he was to prepare. But he does know that his own role is to prepare a path for this mysterious Other, that his whole mission is directed toward him" (14). Ratzinger continues:

All four Gospels describe this mission using a passage from Isaiah: "A voice cries in the wilderness: Prepare the way of the Lord, make straight in the desert a highway for our God" (Is 40:3). Mark adds a compilation of Malachi 3:1 and Exodus 23:20: . . . "Behold, I send my messenger before thy face, who shall prepare thy way" (Mk 1:2). All of these Old Testament texts envisage a saving intervention of God. . . . These ancient words of hope were brought into the present with the Baptist's preaching: great things are about to unfold (14–15).

> Ratzinger picks up on this peculiar stress on the Baptist, musing that he must indeed have created an extraordinary impression (15). He assures us that Mark 1:5 is not an exaggeration: "There went out to him all the country of Judea, and all the people of Jerusalem; and they were baptized by him in the river Jordan" (15). Then, having characterized this as solid historical reporting, he notes that the confession of sins was integral to the rite. The purpose or goal of this is clear, in his view: "truly to leave behind the sinful life one has led until now and to start out on the path to a new, changed life" (15).

What the narrative provides us, that Jesus came from Nazareth and was baptized by John in the Jordan (cf. Mark 1:9), is in fact something new—and consequently of great importance. "So far, nothing has been said about pilgrims from Galilee; the action seemed limited to the region of Judea. The real novelty here is not the fact that Jesus comes from another geographical area, from a distant country, as it were. The real novelty is the fact that he—Jesus—wants to be baptized, that he blends into the gray mass of sinners waiting on the banks of the Jordan" (16).[1]

The theological implication of Jesus' baptism, of course, is that it was an act of "solidarity with men, who have incurred guilt" (17). Yet, the "significance of this event could not fully emerge until it was seen in light of Cross and Resurrection. Descending into the water, the candidates for Baptism confess their sins and seek to be rid of their burden of guilt" (17). Indeed, "[l]ooking at the events in light of the Cross and Resurrection, the Christian people realized what happened; Jesus loaded the burden of all mankind's guilt upon his shoulders; he bore it down into the depths of the Jordan. He inaugurated his public activity by stepping into the place of sinners. His inaugural gesture is an anticipation of the cross" (18).

Therefore, Ratzinger concludes, Jesus "is, as it were, the true Jonah who said to the crew on the ship, 'Take me and throw me into the sea' (Jon 1:12)" (18). Indeed, the "whole significance of Jesus' Baptism . . . first comes to light on the Cross: The Baptism is an acceptance of death for the sins of humanity, and the voice that calls out 'This is my beloved

Son' over the baptismal waters is an anticipatory reference to the Resurrection. This also explains why, in his own discourses [Mark 10:38; Luke 12:50], Jesus uses the word *baptism* to refer to his death" (18).

The Fourth Gospel confirms such an understanding, of course, and portrays the Baptist's response: "Look, the Lamb of God, which takes away the sin of the world" (John 1:29). Ratzinger considers this an authentic utterance of John—historically valid, whether the metaphysics behind the utterance are doctrinal or anachronistic or traditionally based—and finds in it a reference to Isaiah 53:7, in which the Suffering Servant is compared to a lamb led to slaughter (21). "The reference to the Lamb of God interprets Jesus' Baptism, his descent into the abyss of death, as a theology of the Cross" (22).

Whereupon Ratzinger concludes with an overall relation of Jesus' baptism to the progress of his ministry—seeing the course of events that will follow as logically proceeding from this baptismal inauguration:

> I would merely like to underscore briefly three aspects of the scene. The first one is the image of heaven torn open: Heaven stands open above Jesus. His communion with the will of the Father . . . opens heaven, which is essentially the place where God's will is perfectly fulfilled.[2] The next aspect is the proclamation of Jesus' mission by God, by the Father. This proclamation interprets not what Jesus does, but who he is: He *is* the beloved Son on whom God's good pleasure rests. Finally, . . . together with the Son, we encounter the Father and the Holy Spirit. The mystery of the Trinitarian God is beginning to emerge, even though its depths can be fully revealed only when Jesus' journey is complete. For this very reason, though, there is an arc joining this beginning of Jesus' journey and the words with which he sends his disciples into the world after his Resurrection: 'Go therefore and make disciples of all the nations, baptizing them in the name of the Father and of the Son and of the Holy Spirit' (Mt 28:19). The Baptism that Jesus' disciples have been administering since he spoke those words is an entrance into the Master's own Baptism—into the reality that he anticipated by means of it. That is the way to become a Christian. (23)

Ratzinger rejects the idea prominent among liberal theologians that Jesus' baptism was a vocational experience—one to which he felt called and in which he discovered a special relationship to God. His reason: ". . . none of this can be found in the texts" (24) which, he argues, "give us no window into Jesus' inner life. . . . But they do enable us to ascertain how Jesus is connected with 'Moses and the Prophets'; they do enable us to recognize the intrinsic unity of the trajectory stretching from the first moment of his life on the Cross and the Resurrection" (24).

Critique

On p. 15: Ratzinger's thesis that all of Judea, and all the people from Jerusalem had gone out to John to receive the baptism for the forgiveness of sins must be ruled out. If it were true, John must have baptized more than 15,000 people.[3] Clearly the writer is using hyperbole to stress the importance of the event, since it is not factually credible. Moreover, from the practical point of view, it is not very likely that the preaching of John appealed to such numbers, for it was radical—thus dangerous—and disagreeably grim.[4]

On p. 18: Ratzinger's identifying Jesus as "the true Jonah" is an entirely arbitrary act; as an historical statement it is indefensible. Furthermore, the voice at Jesus' baptism—"This is my beloved Son"—is not a divine anticipatory reference to Jesus' resurrection but a structural device—seen as well in Mark 9:7 and Mark 15:39—which will be examined further below (p. 21).

On p. 21: Ratzinger regards John 1:29 as a genuine utterance of the Baptist and accepts its placement in the historical context of Jesus' baptism. But he also considers as factual the dialogue portraying John's humility and Jesus' reassurance with respect to the question of who should be baptizing whom (Matt 3:14–15). Thus he reads these gospel-reports as complementary, even when they are essentially irreconcilable.

But Ratzinger's use of the baptism-event is sufficiently complex that a "simple" list of objections on my part may not be enough to explain the source of my concern. I offer, therefore, a brief analysis of the basic texts about the baptism of Jesus. This will be followed by some historical conclusions that should help to put the Pope's rhetoric in perspective.

Mark 1:9–11
[9]And it happened in those days that Jesus came from Nazareth in Galilee and was baptized in the Jordan by John. [10]And immediately, when he came out of the water, he saw heaven opened and the spirit descend on him like a dove. [11]And a voice rang out from the heavens: "You are my beloved son, in you I am pleased."

This is the earliest extant report of Jesus' baptism. Note that Mark does not state that the purpose of the baptism was to forgive sins (earlier brought out in 1:4: "John the baptizer appeared in the wilderness and preached the baptism of repentance for the forgiveness of sins"). The reason is clear: as the Son of God, Jesus cannot have required such forgiveness. According to Christian belief, he was by definition sinless, because only then could he bear and thus atone for the sins of the world.⁵ In Mark's account, therefore, we find the earliest Christian example of altering the original meaning of Jesus' baptism by John. Indeed, the Gospel of John, the last of the canonical gospels, omits any mention of Jesus' baptism, since it proceeds, as we have said earlier, from a higher Christology. Instead, both John and Jesus are reported as performing baptisms.⁶ Therefore the Markan and the Johannine accounts are contradictory—and one of them has to go if the desire for factual accuracy is sincere.

In Mark's context the baptism of Jesus describes his adoption as Son of God. The baptism scene is literally picked up by 9:7 and 15:39, both of which report occasions when Jesus is proclaimed as Son of God. Thus the story of the baptism is part of a three-fold proclamation of Jesus' divine sonship. This is a literary scheme, and as such it is without any historical value.

Matthew 3:13–15

¹³Then Jesus comes from Galilee to the Jordan to have himself baptized by him. ¹⁴But John sought to prevent him and said, "I need to be baptized by you, and do you come to me?" ¹⁵But Jesus answered and said to him, "Let it be so now, for thus it is fitting for us to fulfill all righteousness." And he let him.

Matthew reworks the text of Mark 1:9. Verse 15 puts a very different "spin" on the account: by getting baptized by John, Jesus will "fulfill all righteousness." He thereby becomes for Matthew a model for his disciples, who must also fulfill all righteousness. Altogether, this author uses "righteousness" seven times,⁷ five of them in the Sermon on the Mount. In the context of the First Gospel we are dealing with what has been called "a human attitude that is supposed to be realized through human deeds."⁸ On this point see especially Matthew 5:20: "Unless your righteousness far exceeds that of the scribes and Pharisees, you will not enter the kingdom of heaven" and Matthew 6:1: "Beware of practicing your righteousness before people to be seen by them; for then you will have no reward from your Father who is in heaven."

Jesus' answer to John is the first word spoken by Jesus in the Gospel of Matthew. It has the character of a signal and points to Matthew 5:17: "Do not think that I have come to abolish the law; I have not come to abolish but to fulfill."

Luke 3:21–22

²¹And it happened, when all the people had themselves baptized, and Jesus had also been baptized and was praying, the heaven was opened, ²²and the holy Spirit descended on him in bodily form, as a

dove, and a voice came from the heaven, "You are my dear son; in you I am well pleased."

Luke reworks Mark 1:9–11; and from the changes he has made one clearly discerns intent. He barely alludes to the baptism of Jesus—which had already led to doctrinal and liturgical confusion among early Christians; instead he mentions it in the context of the entire crowd's participation in the baptism-ritual, and by the time Jesus himself receives baptism John is no longer on the scene, having been apprehended by Herod's men (3:19–22). When in fact Luke does describe the baptism of Jesus, the event is noted in a subordinate clause and overlaid with the mention of Jesus praying,[9] an act which here causes heaven to open.

Verse 23 ("Jesus was, when he appeared, around thirty years old") regards Jesus' baptism as the beginning of his ministry. Thus the report is part of the salvation history inaugurated by God and as such, of course, of dubious historical value.

Nonetheless, the baptism of Jesus by John is in principle historical. Jesus' behavior indicates a view that baptism by John was requisite for his position; but the theological assumptions—the call to fulfill all righteousness, to say nothing of the identification as God's Son—amount to speculative faith statements, since they were unwitnessed, between two men only, or between Jesus and God. They originate with a post-crucifixion Christian community (cf. Gal. 2:20; 4:4) who were retroactively conferring the divine adoption upon Jesus, locating it at the time of his baptism.

THE BOTTOM LINE: Historical-critical work on the baptism-texts disproves Ratzinger's thesis that by means of baptism the sinless Jesus entered into solidarity with sinful humanity, and thus permitted the sins of all humanity to rest upon him.

Chapter Four
on Chapter 2
The Temptations of Jesus

Ratzinger's equivocations transform critical analysis of scripture into doctrinaire support of theological presuppositions.

Overview

According to the synoptic gospels, after Jesus' baptism the Spirit led him into the desert to be tempted by the devil. As Ratzinger explains it, "Jesus has to enter into the drama of human existence, for that belongs to the core of his mission; he has to penetrate it completely, down to its uttermost depths, in order to find the 'lost sheep,' to bear it on his shoulders, and to bring it home" (26). Concerning the brief report of the temptation in Mark 1:13 (Jesus "was in the desert forty days, tempted by the Satan, and he was with the wild beasts, and the angels served him") Ratzinger writes: "Mark brings into relief the parallels between Adam and Jesus, stressing how Jesus 'suffers through' the quintessential human drama.... The desert—the opposite image of the garden— becomes the place of reconciliation and healing" (27).

Before turning to the temptation stories in Matthew and Luke Ratzinger offers a meditation on the general topic. "Constructing a world by our own lights ... while setting God aside as an illusion—that is the temptation that threatens us in many varied forms. Moral posturing is part and parcel of temptation. It does not invite us directly to do evil ... [but rather] pretends to show us a better way.... It claims, moreover, to speak for true realism: What's real is what is right there in front of us—power and bread" (28). But even though "the things of God fade into unreality" (28–29), we discover at last that "God is the issue: Is he real, reality itself, or isn't he? Is he good, or do we have to invent the good ourselves? The God question is the fundamental question, and it sets us down right at the crossroad of human existence" (29).

Ratzinger now turns his attention to the temptation accounts in Matthew and Luke. "What must the Savior of the world do or not do? That is the question the temptations of Jesus are about. The three temptations are identical in Matthew and Luke, but the sequence is different." (29). Ratzinger follows the Matthean order because it builds to a dramatic climax.

Commenting on the statement that Jesus was hungry after his 40-day fast (Matt 4:2), Ratzinger says nothing about the patent impossibility of the statistic, but merely notes the heavy symbolic significance of the number 40 in the Israelite tradition (29). And concerning the tempter's suggestion that Jesus demonstrate his divinity by turning stones to bread (Matt 4:3), Ratzinger writes, "'If you are the Son of God'—we will hear these words again in the mouths of the mocking bystanders at the foot of the Cross.... Mockery and temptation blend into each other here: Christ is being challenged to establish his credibility... a constantly recurring theme in the story of Jesus' life (30).

In the midst of what will be a discussion of the Scriptural breadnarratives—beginning with the exhortation to transform stones into bread—Ratzinger interjects a paragraph on the general topic of world hunger (31), then returns to the texts.

> The first [bread-story] is the multiplication of loaves for the thousands who followed the Lord when he withdrew to a lonely place. Why does Christ now do the very thing he had rejected as a temptation before? The crowds had left everything in order to come hear God's word. They are people who have opened their heart to God and to one another; they are therefore ready to receive the bread with the proper disposition. This miracle of the loaves has three aspects, then. It is preceded by the search for God, for his word, for the teaching that sets the whole of life on the right path. Furthermore, God is asked to supply the bread. Finally, readiness to share with one another is an essential element of the miracle. Listening to God becomes living with God, and leads from faith to love, to the discovery of the other. Jesus is not indifferent toward men's hunger, their bodily needs, but he places these things in the proper context and the proper order. (32)

Once again we are in fact offered a sermon rather than the analysis that the pope has initially promised; for he carefully sidesteps any assessment of the historicity of the incredible events under discussion, instead presenting a clearly theological version of what is otherwise a combination of scientific impossibility and unverifiable narration (no witnesses appear in the desert).

According to Ratzinger, then, the miracle of the loaves serves as a narrative preparation for "the Last Supper, which becomes the Eucharist of the Church and Jesus' perpetual miracle of bread. Jesus himself has become the grain of wheat that died and brought forth much fruit (cf. Jn 12:24). He himself has become bread for us, and *this* multiplication of the loaves endures to the end of time" (32–33). Thus we are able to understand the passage from Deut 8:3, recalled by Jesus when he repudiates the tempter: "Man does not live by bread alone, but . . . by everything that proceeds out of the mouth of the Lord" (33). (All this, of course, hangs on the extraordinary assumption that Jesus said these words to a mythical figure in the presence of a third party who wrote them down or committed them to memory.)

In order to illustrate his last point, Ratzinger adds a critical reflection on the materialism and the atheism of the contemporary Western world:

> The aid offered by the West to developing countries has been purely technically and materially based, and not only has left God out of the picture, but has driven men away from God. And this aid, proudly claiming to "know better," is itself what first turned the "third world" into what we mean today by that term. It has thrust aside indigenous religious, ethical, and social structures and filled the resulting vacuum with its technocratic mind-set. The idea was that we could turn stones into bread. (33)

But history does not operate on a purely material basis, he insists; a greater principle is "the primacy of God. The issue is acknowledging that he is a reality, that he is the reality without which nothing else can be good" (33–34). Only when obedience to the word of God is carried out "does the attitude develop that is also capable of providing bread for all" (34).

Returning to the text, Ratzinger admits that the second temptation is the most difficult for us to understand. According to him "it has to be interpreted as a sort of vision, which once again represents something real, something that poses a particular threat to the man Jesus and his mission. The first point is the striking fact that the devil cites Holy Scripture [Ps 91:11–12] in order to lure Jesus into his trap." (34). Thus the devil proves to be a biblical scholar and plays the theologian.

Here again Ratzinger turns to the present day, noting the Russian writer Vladimir Soloviev's employment of the devil-as-theologian motif in his short story *The Antichrist*. "The Antichrist receives an honorary doctorate in theology from the University of Tübingen and is a great Scripture scholar" (35). To this Ratzinger adds, perhaps tendentiously, "The fact is that scriptural exegesis can become a tool of the Antichrist. Soloviev is not the first person to tell us that; it is the deeper point of the temptation story itself. The alleged findings of scholarly exegesis have been used to put together the most dreadful books that destroy the figure of Jesus and dismantle faith" (35). That could happen, he proposes, because many are reading the Bible with the eyes of a modern human being "whose fundamental dogma is that God cannot act in history—that everything to do with God is to be relegated to the domain of subjectivity" (35). Indeed, he insists, the dispute between Jesus and the devil is an argument over the correct interpretation of scripture and ultimately about who God is, and it therefore remains relevant to all periods of human history. "From this scene on the pinnacle of the Temple, though, we can look out and see the Cross. Christ did not cast himself down from the pinnacle of the Temple. He did not leap into the abyss. He did not tempt God. But he did descend into the abyss of death" (37–38).[1]

Moving on to the third temptation, Ratzinger asserts that it constitutes the climax of the narrative.

> The devil takes the Lord in a vision onto a high mountain. He shows him all the kingdoms of the earth and their splendor and offers him kingship over the world. Isn't that precisely the mission of the Messiah? Isn't he supposed to be the king of the world who unifies the whole earth in one great kingdom of peace and well-being? We saw that the temptation to turn stones into bread has two remarkable counterparts later on in Jesus' story: the multiplication of the loaves and the Last Supper. The same thing is true here. (38)

The first "counterpart" to be identified is Jesus' statement in Matt 28:18 that "all authority in heaven and on earth has been given to me": the second is the power that accrues to him as a result of the resurrection that follows his death on the other mountain, Golgotha.

After dealing with these two "counterparts" and the Church's embrace of power and struggle for freedom—"the struggle to avoid identifying Jesus' Kingdom with any political structure" (40), Ratzinger comes to Barabbas—the man Pilate reportedly offered to release in place of Jesus. Quite without surprise Ratzinger accepts the historical veracity of this character in the story. "The choice of Jesus versus Barabbas is not accidental; two messiah figures, two forms of messianic belief stand in opposition. This becomes even clearer when we consider that the name Bar-Abbas means 'son of the father.' This is a typically messianic appellation, the cultic name of a prominent leader of the messianic movement. The last great Jewish messianic war was fought in the year 132 by Bar-Kokhba, 'son of the star.' The form of the name is the same, and it stands for the same intention" (40–41).

Ratzinger proceeds to a remarkable present-day extrapolation that is worth considering in full:

> If we had to choose today, would Jesus of Nazareth, the son of Mary, the Son of the Father, have a chance? Do we really know Jesus at all? Do we understand him? Do we not perhaps have to make an effort, today as always, to get to know him all over again? The tempter is not so crude as to suggest to us directly that we should worship the devil. He merely suggests that we opt for the reasonable decision,

that we choose to give priority to a planned and thoroughly organized world, where God may have his place as a private concern but must not interfere in our essential purposes. Soloviev attributes to the Antichrist a book entitled *The Open Way to World Peace and Welfare*. This book becomes something of a new Bible, whose real message is the worship of well-being and rational planning. (41)

What follows next is a discussion of Peter's messianic confession at Caesarea Philippi (the Matthean version). "Peter, speaking in the name of the disciples, has confessed that Jesus is the Messiah-Christ, the Son of the Living God. In doing so, he has expressed in words the faith that builds up the Church and inaugurates the new community of faith based on Christ" (42). Yet in the next moment Jesus defines "Messiah" in terms of the cross, and Peter, protesting against this concept, is rejected as Satan (Matt 16:22–23).

For Ratzinger, the Satanic temptation faced by Jesus at Caesarea Philippi corresponds to the modern form of the same temptation: to see "Christianity as a recipe for progress and the proclamation of universal prosperity and the proclamation of universal prosperity as the real goal of all religions, including Christianity" (42–43). Yet in sharp contrast to this, Jesus embodies the suffering Servant who, through humiliation and physical pain, in fact offers salvation (cf. Luke 24:25) and today in essence "repeats to us what he said in reply to Satan, what he said to Peter, and what he explained further to the disciples in Emmaus: No kingdom of this world is the Kingdom of God, the total condition of mankind's salvation. Earthly kingdoms remain earthly human kingdoms" (43–44).

Next Ratzinger addresses the great question with which he confronts his readers throughout the book—only because he has patently got the answer: "[I]f not world peace, universal prosperity, and a better world" (44), what has Jesus brought? His answer is simple, predictable, and direct:

> [Jesus] has brought God. He has brought the God who formerly unveiled his countenance gradually, first to Abraham, then to Moses and the Prophets, and then in the Wisdom Literature—the God who revealed his face only in Israel, even though he was also honored among the pagans in various shadowy guises. It is this God, the God of Abraham, Isaac, and Jacob, the true God, whom he has brought to the nations of the earth. (44)

Critique

On pp. 25–31: Given Ratzinger's avowed respect for the historical method, he surely should have admitted the 40-day fast to be mythic fiction—or at least an analogy of sorts, with literary significance. Refraining from such an honest (and potentially helpful) explanation, however, he merely conjures up a picture of the early church-leaders' "stretching number symbolism in an admittedly slightly playful way" (29). This bit of exegetical "playfulness" results unfortunately in further obfuscation and denial of theological posturing.

On p. 32: According to the New Testament gospels, the story of the multiplication of loaves is not preceded by the search for God, for his word, or for the teaching that sets the whole of life on the right path; nor is God asked to supply the bread, nor is readiness to share with one another an essential element of the story, nor does it contain significant eucharistic elements. In what follows Ratzinger offers us another lengthy sermon that combines a number of motifs whose relevance to the subject at hand derives more from the preacher's imaginative powers than from scholarly insight or analysis. Once again any pretense of dealing with the historicity of the story or the life of Jesus of Nazareth is startling in its absence.

For the sake of further clarification, we may consider a brief exegesis of the two stories of the multiplication of the loaves in the Gospel of Mark—first, the five thousand, and second, the four thousand.

Mark 6:34–44

The Feeding of the Five Thousand

[34]And when he got out, he saw a great crowd of people and he had pity on them, for they were like sheep without a shepherd, and he began to teach them many things. [35]And when the hour was already advanced, his disciples came to him and said, "The place is lonely and the hour is already advanced. [36]Send them away, so that they can go into the neighboring places and villages and can buy something to eat!" [37]But he answered and said to them, "You give them something to eat!" And they say to him, "Shall we go off and buy bread for 200 denarii and give them something to eat?" [38]But he said to them, "How much bread do you have? Go and see!" And they looked and say, "Five loaves and two fishes." [39]And he commanded them all to settle them down by companies on the green grass. [40]And they settled down, in groups by hundreds and by fifties. [41]And he took the loaves and the two fishes and looked up to heaven, gave thanks, and broke the loaves and gave them to his disciples, to give to them, and he shared out the two fishes for all. [42]And all ate and were filled, [43]and they took the fragments, twelve baskets full, also of the fishes. [44]And there were five thousand men who ate.

Verse 34a proceeds of course from vv 32–33, in which the presence of the crowd of people for this mass feeding is arranged by a stroke of

Markan literary manipulation. And, as in Mark 6:6, verse 34b shows Jesus teaching; it is a typical scene in this gospel. Verse 37 (of the above passage), with its command that the disciples provide the necessary food, coupled with their puzzled reaction, recalls in part 5:31, when they are stunned that Jesus could identify a single touch from among the throngs surrounding him. It is another expression of their incomprehension, and therefore is all but certain to have been inserted by the author, who is stressing the ignorance of the disciples. It would follow, then, that Mark most likely did not envision the feeding narratives in high-Christological terms of the Eucharist. For him this is simply one more miracle that he later interprets (6:52; 8:14–21) as a depiction of the disciples' lack of understanding.

The event in vv 34–44 is commonly referred-to as a "gift miracle," with the narration following that genre's standard pattern. First, it depicts need (lack of food, vv 35–38); second, the need is removed by Jesus, who miraculously satisfies many with what little is on hand (vv 39–42); third, the miracle is confirmed by the reference to the leftovers (v 43); and finally, we are reminded once again of the enormous number who were fed (v 44).

For its essential content, the narrative is indebted to 2 Kgs 4:42–44, in which Elisha feeds 100 men with only 20 loaves—although, typically, Jesus far surpasses Elisha. The green grass of vv 39–40 may reflect Ps 23:2, and in the dividing into groups we hear an echo of Exod 18:25.

The composition of the narrative reflects the literary tradition of the Christian community, whose members saw material needs being fulfilled in Jesus. Jesus had aroused the expectation among his disciples that the hungry would be fed (Luke 6:21) and that all who belong to God's kingdom would be gathered together as at a large banquet (Matt 8:11–12). Against such a background, the story of an actual feeding of a multitude easily enough developed.

Mark 8:1–9

The Feeding of the Four Thousand

[1]In those days, when again a great crowd of people was present and they had nothing to eat, he called the disciples and says to them, [2]"I have compassion for the people, because they have persisted with me now for three days and have nothing to eat. [3]And if I sent them away hungry, they will faint on the way. And some of them have come from afar." [4]And his disciples answered him, "How can anyone feed these people with loaves here in the wilderness?" [5]And he asked them, "How many loaves do you have?" and they answered, "Seven." [6]And he commands the crowd to lie down on the ground. And he took the seven loaves, gave thanks, and broke and gave them to his disciples,

to set them before them, and they gave (them) to the people. ⁷They also had a few small fish; and after he spoke the thanksgiving over them, he told the disciples to set these before them as well. ⁸And they ate and were satisfied; and they took up the fragments which remained, seven baskets. ⁹Now there were about four thousand. And he sent them away.

Only Mark gives two accounts of the feeding. The first version (6:34–44) takes place on Jewish soil, while this second one occurs in Gentile territory. Mark's purpose emerges unequivocally from Jesus' ministering to Jews and Gentiles. The most important differences between the second story and the first are that (1) its style is more terse; (2) it is Jesus rather than the disciples who recognizes the need of the crowds; (3) the disciples have seven loaves rather than five; (4) 4000 are fed, rather than 5000, and seven baskets remain rather than twelve; (5) Jesus initiates his compassionate action on the basis of physical need, whereas in the previous story, it was their spiritual need that was emphasized from the outset; and (6) the role of the disciples is recognizably diminished.

The tradition behind the second account reveals it to be a version of the same "event," as opposed to a second "event" in its own right that happened to resemble the first. By comparison with the tradition behind 6:34–44, the tradition reflected in 8:1–9 appears to reflect two priorities: first, there is no substantial redactional expansion at the beginning; second, we find in v 3 no mention of nearby farms and villages.

Nevertheless, 8:1–9 is secondary to 6:34–44 because it emphasizes Jesus' active role: its action begins with the initiative of Jesus (vv 1–2); the description 'He had compassion' (6:34) has become the direct speech "I have compassion" (8:2); and the request of the disciples (6:36) has been changed into Jesus' assessment of the situation (8:3).

Surely it is a serious omission on the part of the commentator that he has ignored basic issues of textual analysis in favor of an almost exclusively homiletic or preaching stance.

On p. 35: Ratzinger complains that people these days read the Bible with the assumption that God has never really entered into human history. To be sure, that is the consensus among scholars in all academic areas. Not only is this an intellectually sound premise, but it also amounts to a methodological non-theism that is entirely divorced from dogmatics. Non-theism is distinct from atheism, in the same way that historical criticism, by definition, is distinct from faith-based reception. Yet Ratzinger's closed system of thought has no room for such a logical differentiation, and as a result he condemns any modern form of inquiry that so much as questions religious claims of inerrancy and ultimate truth. Let me hasten to add that, as Lloyd Geering has demonstrated, it is precisely such a "godless" attitude—and not Christian absolutist faith—that has opened the way for religious freedom and tolerance.[2]

On pp. 40–41: Inasmuch as the scene in which Barabbas appears is almost certainly fictional and no available sources support a messianic characterization of the name (which simply indicates "the son of his father" and was far from uncommon), we have no reason to suppose that we are dealing with a messianic contender here. After all, Simon Peter's Aramaic name was Bar-Jona (Matt 16:17), and the magician who supposedly met Paul on Cyprus (Acts 13:6) was called Bar-Jesus. Yet nobody has ever imagined a messianic connotation with respect to either of the two or with other persons of similar names.[3] Ratzinger's reference to Bar-Kochba, who at the beginning of the second century was regarded as a messiah, proves nothing; his name alludes to Num 24:17, whereas the name Bar-Abbas involves no reference to Scripture at all.

THE BOTTOM LINE: By ad hoc, thematic associations and verbal manipulation, Ratzinger manages to use the Bible to support his preconceived theological stance. This stands in stark contrast to his promise in the Preface—for instead of supplementing historical criticism with theological method, he is in effect repudiating modern biblical scholarship with wanton subjectivity.

Chapter Five
on Chapter 3
The Gospel of the Kingdom of God

Contrary to Ratzinger's tortured exegesis, Jesus' message does not identify the kingdom of God with his own person.

Overview

Ratzinger begins the chapter by examining the meaning of the word "gospel," by which Mark and Matthew identify the preaching of Jesus (46). He correctly suggests that "Good News," the common modern translation of the Greek noun *euanggelion*, "falls far short of the order of magnitude of what is actually meant by the word" (46). He then asserts—this time incorrectly—that the word comes from the cult "of the Roman emperors who understood themselves as lords, saviors, and redeemers of the world. The messages issued by the emperor were called in Latin *evangelium*, regardless of whether or not their content was particularly cheerful and pleasant. The idea was that what comes from the emperor is a saving message, that is not just a piece of news, but a change in the world for the better" (46–47). The evangelists therefore took up this noun in order to express the idea that "[w]hat the emperors, who pretend to be gods, illegitimately claim, really occurs here—a message endowed with plenary authority, a message that is not just talk, but reality" (47).

As Ratzinger sees it, the main import of the term "gospel" is that the "Kingdom of God is at hand.... This announcement is the actual core of Jesus' words and works.... [W]hereas the axis of Jesus' preaching before Easter is the Kingdom of God, Christology is the center of the preaching of the Apostles after Easter" (47–48).

He asks whether the latter point means "that there has been a falling away from the real preaching of Jesus" (48). In a keen rhetorical move the pope here introduces the pithy statement of Catholic modernist[1] Alfred Loisy (1857–1940) who had offered a somewhat jocular but substantive answer to the question when he described the situation in his now famous saying, "Jesus preached the Kingdom of God, and what came was the Church."[2] The words contain irony, but certainly reflect sadness as well. "Instead of the great expectation of God's own Kingdom, of a new world transformed by God himself, we got something quite different—and what a pathetic substitute it is: the Church" (48).

This disingenuous confession quickly gives way to what our author considers a far more important issue: the relation of the preaching to the preacher. Was Jesus "just a messenger charged with representing a cause that is ultimately independent of him, or is the messenger himself the message?" (49). Ratzinger seeks to finesse the issue of the church: "The basic question is actually about the relationship between the Kingdom of God and Christ. It is on this that our understanding of the Church will depend" (49).

Catholic theology of the nineteenth and early twentieth centuries, he proposes, had brought Kingdom of God and Church into close proximity; the Church was more or less the Kingdom of God on earth. "By that time, however, the Enlightenment had sparked an exegetical revolution in Protestant theology, and one of the main results of this revolution was an innovative understanding of Jesus' message concerning the Kingdom of God. This new interpretation immediately broke up into very different trends, however" (50–51).

One major trend in the new Protestant thought came in the figure and work of Adolf von Harnack (1851–1930), and he directed his conclusions against the collectivity as well as the heteronomous, ritualized indoctrination found in Judaism and Catholicism. "This antithesis between ritual and morality, between the collective and the individual remained influential long after Harnack's time, and it was widely adopted in Catholic exegesis from about the 1930s on" (51).

The age of liberal theology ended with the First World War. Yet long before that, Ratzinger argues, an intellectual revolution had become visible. "The first clear signal of what was to come was a book by Johannes Weiss that appeared in 1892 under the title *Jesus' Proclamation of the Kingdom of God*. . . . Jesus' message, it was now claimed, was radically 'eschatological'; his proclamation of the imminent Kingdom of God was a proclamation of the imminent end of the world, of the inbreaking of a new world where, as the term *kingdom* suggests, God would reign" (52). Even so-called "growth parables," he asserts disapprovingly—Mark 4:3–9; 4:26–29; 4:30–32; Matt 13:33; Luke 13:20–21—that obviously disagree with the eschatological view were nonetheless made to fit into this thematic reading. Ratzinger continues in bold condemnation of both the blindness of the interpreters and the wantonness of their chosen method: "The point, it was said, is not growth; rather, Jesus is trying to say that while now our world is small, something very different is about to burst suddenly onto the scene. Here, obviously, theory predominated over listening to the text" (52).

Furthermore, insists Ratzinger, turning to a broader complaint, the secular reinterpretations of the Kingdom of God are to be rejected as not only utopian but responsible for the marginalization of God, whose existence is discredited to the level of a nuisance. "Faith and religions are now directed toward political goals. Only the organization of the world counts. Religion only matters insofar as it can serve that objective. The post-Christian vision of faith and religion is disturbingly close to Jesus' third temptation" (54–55).

The solution, for Ratzinger, is a return "to the Gospel, the real Jesus" (55). The implication of this return to or recovery of "the real Jesus" is a reconsideration of what is meant by the Kingdom, in Jesus' view—that is, "not an imminent or yet to be established 'kingdom,' but God's actual sovereignty over the world, which is becoming an event in history in a new way" (55). To put it more plainly: "When Jesus speaks of the Kingdom of God, he is quite simply proclaiming God, and proclaiming him to be the living God, who is able to act concretely in the world and in history and is even now so acting" (55). Ratzinger backs this up with reference to the Hebrew, in which *malkut* (kingdom) is an action word describing the royal functioning of the king. Jesus is telling us about a dynamic God operating within his Kingdom. "'God exists' and 'God is really God'," Jesus states simply; "he holds in his hands the threads of the world. In this sense, Jesus' message is very simple and thoroughly God-centered" (55–56).

Ratzinger considers Jesus a "true Israelite." Indeed, "in terms of the inner dynamic promises made to Israel—he transcended Judaism" (57). Thus we have "something new, . . . something that finds expression above all in such statements as 'the Kingdom of God is at hand' (Mk 1:15), it 'has already come upon you' (Mt 12:28), it is 'in the midst of you (Lk 17:21). What these words express is a process of coming that has already begun and extends over the whole of history" (57–58). The apocalyptic or eschatological interpretation of these kingdom-images is not convincing for Ratzinger; as he puts it, "if we consider the entire corpus of Jesus' sayings, it can actually be decisively ruled out. This is evident from the fact that the exponents of the apocalyptic interpretation of Jesus' Kingdom proclamation (i.e., imminent expectation) are simply forced, on the basis of their hypothesis, to ignore a large number of Jesus' sayings on this matter, and to bend others violently in order to make them fit" (58).

To defend his point Ratzinger lists three aspects of Jesus' message regarding the Kingdom:

The first aspect deals with its disarmingly small proportions: "its meager dimensions within history. It is like a grain of mustard, the tiniest of all seeds [Mark 4:30–32]. It is like a leaven, a small quantity in comparison to the whole mass of the dough, yet decisively important for what becomes of the dough [Matt 13:33/Luke 13:20–21]. It is compared again and again to the seed that is planted in the field of the world, where it meets various fates—it is pecked up by the birds, or it is suffocated among the thorns, or else it ripens into abundant fruit [Mark 4:3–8]. Another parable tells of how the seed of the Kingdom grows, but an enemy comes and sows weeds in its midst, which for the present grow up with the seed, and the division coming only at the end (cf. Mt 13:24–30)" (58).

The second aspect of the Kingdom's perplexity appears in its hidden nature. In Matt 13:44, Jesus "compares it with a treasure that was buried in the field. The finder of the treasure buries it again and sells everything in order to buy the field, so to gain possession of the treasure that can fulfill every desire" (58–59). What follows immediately (Matt 13:45–46) is "a parallel to this in the parable of the pearl of great price, whose finder likewise gives away everything[3] in order to attain this good of surpassing value" (59).

The third aspect of the Kingdom comes to light in Matt 11:12 when Jesus makes the enigmatic statement that 'the kingdom of heaven has suffered violence and men of violence take it by force'" (59).

Thus, the reality that Jesus refers to as both "'Kingdom of God, lordship of God' is extremely complex, and only by accepting it in its entirety can we gain access to, and let ourselves be guided by, his message" (59).

Finally, Ratzinger returns to the intriguing problem inherent in the Kingdom-image: are we to see Jesus as messenger or as message? On the basis of Luke 17:20–21 ("The Kingdom of God is not coming with signs to be observed . . . for behold, the Kingdom of God is in the midst of you") and 11:20 ("But if it is by the finger of God that I cast out demons, then the Kingdom of God has come upon you"), Ratzinger concludes, it "is not simply in Jesus' physical presence that the 'Kingdom' is located; rather, it is in his action, accomplished in the Holy Spirit" (60). Therefore one must say, "The new proximity of the Kingdom of which Jesus speaks—the distinguishing feature of his message—is to be found in Jesus himself. . . . [I]n this context we also understand his invitation to follow him courageously, leaving everything else behind. He himself is the treasure; communion with him is the pearl of great price" (60–61).

Since the "Kingdom of God" pervades Jesus' proclamation, Ratzinger concludes, one must understand it as both background and content of Jesus' overall preaching. And in the next chapter, he continues, this proclamation will be discussed fully; for the subject will be the Sermon on the Mount, one of the core demonstrations of Jesus' message. It will also reveal Jesus' status that he "always speaks as the Son, that the relation between Father and Son is always present as the background of his message. In this sense, God is always at the center of the discussion, yet precisely because Jesus himself is God—the Son—his entire preaching is a message about the mystery of his person, it is Christology, that is, discourse concerning God's presence in his own action and being" (63). From this, according to Ratzinger, derives the demand for a decision on our part, a commitment "that leads to the Cross and Resurrection" (63).

Critique

On pp. 46–47: Mark did not employ the noun "gospel" to express resistance to the Emperor cult, but rather to denote the primitive Christian preaching that proclaimed the death and resurrection of Jesus.[4] Paul similarly understood the term when he experienced his call (around 33 CE).[5] This is abundantly clear from an analysis of the following passage:

> *1 Corinthians 15:1–5*
> [1]And now, brothers, I must remind you of the gospel that I preached to you; the gospel which you received, in which you stand, [2]by which you are saved, if you hold fast—unless you believed in vain. [3]For I delivered to you as of first importance what I also received:
>
>> That Christ died for our sins in accordance with the scriptures [4]and that he was buried; that he has been raised on the third day in accordance with the scriptures; [5]and that he appeared to Cephas, then to the Twelve.

In verse 3a, then, Paul unmistakably declares that he received a "gospel," he transmitted this to the Corinthians, and that it likely took place when he founded their community (see verse 1). This gospel consists of the elements quoted in vv 3b–5, which he adds here in order to remind the Corinthians of what he had told them.

It is not very likely that the Christians from whom Paul had received the basics of Christianity borrowed the word "gospel" from the Emperor-cult simply to deploy it in opposition to that cult. Moreover, we have no record of a technical use of the term "gospel" in the Emperor cult; and in fact the actual origin of the term has not yet been ascertained.[6]

On p. 48: That Ratzinger misunderstands Alfred Loisy is surprising. That is, modernism was once one of the main topics of discussion in the Catholic Church, and thus a subject the present pope should know well. Yet not only does he fail to refer directly to Loisy's book; it appears as though he has not read it.

When Loisy quipped, "Jesus foretold the kingdom, and it was the Church that came,"[7] he was trying to shed light on the problem of Jesus' relationship to the church that had claimed to represent him and thus his authority. Generations of scholars after Loisy, however, interpreted the sentence in a jocular way, to mean that the Catholic church was an aberration from Jesus' gospel. Loisy in fact thought otherwise. Indeed, he wrote in defense of the Church, and against his contemporary, Adolf Harnack of the University of Berlin, who maintained that the institution had betrayed its birthright.[8] A continuation of Loisy's statement makes his real intention clear:

> [The Church] came, enlarging the form of the gospel, which it was impossible to preserve as it was, as soon as the Passion closed the ministry of Jesus. There is no institution on the earth or in history whose status and value may not be questioned if the principle is established that nothing may exist except in its original form. Such a principle is contrary to the law of life, which is movement and a continual effort of adaptation to conditions always new and perpetually changing. Christianity has not escaped this law, and cannot be reproached for submission to it. It could not do otherwise than it has done.[9]

It is clear, then, that Ratzinger has misrepresented if not misunderstood Loisy's point. This of course defeats his argument entirely.

On pp. 52 and 57–60: In these two sections, Ratzinger both paraphrases and characterizes a number of parables, but does not go into exegetical details necessary to validate his argument. Moreover, he refuses to imagine, let alone acknowledge, the inauthenticity of a single parable, so that dialogue on historicity, which was at the outset part of his intention, is out of the question. In so doing, he forfeits the right to criticize scholars, for he is effectively refusing to enter into a discussion with them.

To help elucidate this point—and at the same time prepare the way for further examination of Ratzinger's take on Jesus' parables, it will be useful to demonstrate this concept of inauthenticity.

Matthew 13:24–30

The weeds among the wheat[10]

[24]The kingdom of heaven is like a man who sowed good seed in his field. [25]But while the people were sleeping, his enemy came and

> sowed weeds among the wheat and went away. ²⁶And when the plants grew and bore fruit the weeds also appeared. ²⁷And the servants of the householder came and said to him, "Lord, did you not sow good seed on the field? How then does it now have weeds?" ²⁸And he said to them, "An enemy has done this." And the servants said to him, "Then do you want us to go and gather them?" ²⁹But he said, "No, lest in gathering the weeds at the same time you tear up the roots of the wheat. ³⁰Let both grow together until the harvest; and at harvest time I will say to the reapers. 'First gather the wheat and bind it in bundles to burn it; but gather the wheat into my barns.'"

This parable stands in the place of the parable of the seed growing by itself (Mark 4:26–30), which Matthew has, no doubt deliberately, omitted. The present parable shares with its Markan counterpart the theme of non-intervention in the process of growth between sowing and harvest. But it differs from Mark 4:26–30 in that here we have not a natural occurrence, but a hostile individual action by which Matthew seeks to inculcate his oft-repeated insistence that despite the "sowing" of the kingdom of God, evil remains present—even in the Christian community. At the same time this indicates that the parable is dramatizing experiences of the young community in combating the "the evil one" ("the enemy" is clearly an image for the devil—see Mark 4:15) and counsels patience. At this decisive point, then, the parable becomes a mere allegory.

The parable is inauthentic, since it reflects a situation in the post-Easter community. Moreover, the historical Jesus reported a vision of the devil's fall from power (Luke 10:18), and so can hardly have credited his influence as highly as does the present parable.[11]

Mark 4:3–20

The parable of the sower and its interpretation

In Mark 4:3–8 Jesus tells the following parable:

> ³Listen: A sower went out to sow. ⁴And it happened that while he was sowing some seed fell on the pathway, and the birds came and devoured it. ⁵And other fell on the rock, where it did not have much earth, and it immediately sprang up, because it had no deep earth. ⁶But when the sun rose, it was scorched, and because it had no root, it withered. ⁷And other fell among the thorns, and the thorns grew up and choked it, and it bore no fruit. ⁸And other fell on the good earth and bore fruit, growing and increasing until it bore thirty- and sixty- and one hundredfold.

The interpretation given by Jesus to his puzzled listeners shortly afterwards (Mark 4:14–20) reads:

> ¹⁴The sower sows the *word*. ¹⁵And these are the ones on the pathway where the *word* is sown and when they hear, Satan immediately comes and takes away the *word* that has been sown in them. ¹⁶And these are those who are sown on the rocks who, when they hear the *word*, immediately receive it with joy, ¹⁷but have no roots in themselves, for they are people of the moment. When tribulation or persecution for the *word*'s sake arises, they fall away. ¹⁸And others are those sown in the thorns. These are those who hear the *word*, ¹⁹but then the cares of this world, and the deceit of riches, and the desire for other things enter them and choke the *word*, and it fails to yield. ²⁰And those are the ones sown on good earth, who hear and receive the *word* and bear fruit, thirty- and sixty- and one hundredfold.

Although the parable itself is arguably authentic the subsequent interpretation cannot be attributed to Jesus. First, it is indelibly stamped with Christian terminology. For example, the term "the word" is a characteristic designation first used in the primitive church to indicate the gospel-message. In keeping with this, vv 14–20 contain several statements about the word that are alien to Jesus' preaching but common in a later period: the preacher spreads the word; the word is received with joy; persecution arises because of the word; the word grows; the word brings forth fruit.

A second reason why the interpretation in Mark 4:14–20 cannot go back to Jesus is that words occurring in this text do not appear elsewhere in the first three gospels, but are common in the rest of the New Testament literature: e.g. "sow" in the sense of "proclaim" and "root" used to signify inner steadfastness.

Third, in addition to these linguistic points another crucial point is that the interpretation of the parable does not match the original story, for the seed that was originally the word sown on different kinds of ground has now become different kinds of people. Furthermore, the parable has been shifted in a psychological direction, so that it is now an admonition to the newly converted to examine their hearts to see whether they have been truly converted.

One is therefore compelled to conclude that Mark 4:14–20, the interpretation of the parable of the sower, comes from the primitive church, which saw this parable as an allegory and expounded it accordingly, feature by feature. The seed is the gospel message preached by the early church, and a somewhat awkwardly expressed metaphor presents four types of soil as four kinds of people. Clearly, two quite different images have been combined: the gospel as God's seed, and human beings as God's field.

Here then is a clear case in which words are attributed to Jesus when in fact he could not have uttered them. That being the case, one is led to ask how many similar passages exist—and, as a corollary, what percentage of Jesus' reported sayings are in fact authentic?

The question becomes more urgent when we consider the wider context in which the parable and its interpretation stand. Between the parable of the sower and its interpretation, we find the following curious explanation of Jesus' choice to speak in parables.

Mark 4:10–12
[10]And when he was alone, those around him along with the Twelve asked him about the parables. [11]And he said to them, "To you is given the mystery of the kingdom of god. But to those outside everything happens in parables, [12]that

'seeing they may see and yet not perceive
and hearing they may not hear and yet not understand,
lest they repent and be forgiven' [Isa 6:9–10]."

In short, we are told that Jesus speaks in parables with the express aim of preventing the hearers from being converted and forgiven (v 12). The contradiction between this statement and Jesus' real intention could not be greater. Whereas it cannot be doubted that Jesus spoke in parables in order to be better understood, the author of vv 10–12 makes him say quite the opposite: he has spoken in parables in order to be "misunderstood," in order to mislead "those outside."

This so-called "theory of hardening," which here is placed on the lips of Jesus himself, goes back to the author of the Gospel of Mark or one of his sources, with whose point of view the author concurred. The statement in vv 11–12, the second part of which is a quotation of Isa 6:9–10, must be seen in the context of other passages that refer to Israel's unbelief. One thinks of the decision of the Pharisees and Herodians to kill Jesus (Mark 3:6), the Pharisees' request for a sign (8:11), the question about Jesus' authority put by the high priests and scribes (11:27–33), and the rejection of the evil tenants who slew the son of the vineyard owner (Mark 12:9). Here, of course we must recall the destruction of Jerusalem in the year 70 CE—just before Mark wrote his Gospel—in order to understand the emphatic nature of this last passage.

The saying in vv 11–12 can be seen to correspond to Peter's messianic declaration (Mark 8:29) and the confession of the centurion under the cross (15:39). According to Mark, both figures have recognized the mystery of the kingdom of God.

These examples will suffice to demonstrate how sayings attributed to Jesus are in fact interpretations for which the interpreters sought to gain greater authority by assigning them to Jesus. Naturally, this has made it difficult for later readers of the Bible to arrive at historical truth, since any serious attempts to discover whether these are really sayings of Jesus has been directly or indirectly obstructed by those who assert the special status of the Bible as Holy Scripture.

On pp. 57–58: Ratzinger claims that, in view of the entire corpus of Jesus' sayings, he clearly had no imminent apocalyptic expectation. Nevertheless, two important observations suggest the possibility of such teachings.

First, Jesus belongs to a movement chronologically midway between John the Baptist (precursor) and the apostle Paul (promoter). Since both John and Paul clearly expressed belief in the imminent end,[12] it is reasonable to suppose that Jesus might have shared their outlook.

Second, Jesus' preaching of forthcoming judgment supports the same conclusion. Note, for example, Luke 17:34–35 (and Matt 24:40–41): [34]"I tell you, in that night, there will be two in one bed; one will be taken, the other left. [35]There will be two women grinding at the same place, one will be taken, the other left."[13]

> **THE BOTTOM LINE:** The assertion that Jesus' statements about the kingdom of God contain a mysteriously hidden message about himself is based on a series of textual distortions. Bluntly put, nowhere does Jesus identify the kingdom of God with his own person.[14]

Chapter Six
on Chapter 4
The Sermon on the Mount

To be sure, Jesus' Sermon on the Mount updates the Torah; but nowhere in it, Ratzinger notwithstanding, does he claim divine status.

After a brief introduction to the Sermon on the Mount (64–70), this fourth chapter goes on to deal with the Beatitudes (70–99), and the Torah of the Messiah (99–127).

Overview of pp. 64–70

Ratzinger's introduction to Matthew 5–7 — commonly known as the Sermon on the Mount — consists of a mixture of exegetical and meditative remarks. As he notes at the outset, "[f]rom the start of his Gospel, Matthew claims the Old Testament for Jesus, even when it comes to apparent minutiae" (64). His explains his reasoning as follows: "With a few strokes of his brush — in fourteen verses (4:12–25) — Matthew presents his audience with an initial portrait of the figure and work of Jesus. Thereupon follow the three chapters of the Sermon on the Mount. What is this sermon? With this great discourse, Matthew puts together a picture of Jesus as the new Moses" (65). And he ends this section with a reminder to the reader that the construal of "disciple" is not to be restricted to those who heard that Sermon; that is, "Everyone who hears and accepts the word can become a 'disciple'" (66).

Then follow meditations on the mountain itself — its symbolic relation to Moses' Sinai, the mountaintop vision of Elijah, and the wonderful transformation it bespeaks. "God's power is now revealed in his mildness, his greatness in his simplicity and closeness.... What formerly found expression in storm, fire, and earthquake now takes on the form of the Cross, of the suffering God who calls us to step into this mysterious fire, the fire of crucified love...." (67) Whereupon Ratzinger extends his textual interpretation to what must be recognized as a sermon-fragment:

Now God speaks intimately, as one man to another. Now he descends into the depth of their human sufferings. Yet that very act prompts, and will continually prompt, his hearers—the hearers who nonetheless think of themselves as disciples—to say, "This is a hard saying; who can listen to it?" (Jn 6:60). This new goodness of the Lord is no sugarplum. The scandal of the Cross is harder for many to bear than the thunder of Sinai had been for the Israelites. In fact, the Israelites were quite right when they said that they would die if God should speak with them (Ex 20:19). Without a "dying," without the demise of what is simply our own, there is no communion with God and no redemption. Our meditation on the Baptism has already demonstrated this for us—Baptism cannot be reduced to mere ritual. (67–68)

Having laid the foundations for future discussion, Ratzinger reiterates what he assumes he has proven: "It should be clear by now that the Sermon of the Mount is the new Torah brought by Jesus" (68). And he draws the narrative comparison: "Moses could deliver his Torah only by entering into the divine darkness on the mountain. Jesus' Torah likewise presupposes his entering into communion with the Father, the inward ascents of his life, which are then prolonged in his descents into communion of life and suffering with men" (68).

Critique

On pp. 64–70: This poetic prolegomenon provides little or no insight into the purported subject of this book—the life of Jesus of Nazareth. It is a personal expression of faith that cannot be subjected to any degree of scientific scrutiny.

On p. 68: Ratzinger's understanding of the Sermon of the Mount as the new Torah brought by Jesus is an overtly Christian interpretation of Judaism. Later (99–112) he deals with the "Torah of the Messiah," which is supposedly identical with the new Torah. But for Judaism, the idea of a new Torah is not only unacceptable but also unnecessary. According to the Rabbis, God revealed Torah on Mount Sinai; indeed, before the creation he had already established it. Its revelation to Moses was final, without need of further disclosure.[1]

Overview of pp. 70–99
The Beatitudes

Ratzinger starts by rejecting the view that the Beatitudes—all of which he attributes to the historical Jesus—in any way contradict the Ten Commandments. Rather, Matt 5:17–18 purports to show that Jesus has reinforced the Commandments (70–71).[2]

The Beatitudes, he says, are a series of paradoxes. "It is precisely those who are poor in worldly terms, those thought of as lost souls, who are the truly fortunate ones" (71). Further, these are "eschatological promises. This must not, however, be taken to mean that the joy they proclaim is postponed until some infinitely remote future or applies exclusively to the next world" (72). In fact, from the moment when a human being "begins to see and to live from God's perspective, when he is a companion on Jesus' way, then he lives by new standards, and something of the *éschaton*, of the reality to come, is already present. Jesus brings joy in the midst of affliction" (72).

As paradoxes, the Beatitudes express the believer's reality "in the world in similar terms to those repeatedly used by Paul[3] to describe his experience of living and suffering as an Apostle" (72). They express exactly what John in another way displays in calling "the Lord's Cross an 'exaltation,' an elevation to God's throne on high" (73).

Thus, for Ratzinger, the Beatitudes show what it means to be a disciple. "They become more concrete and real the more completely the disciple dedicates himself to service in a way that is illustrated for us in the life of Saint Paul" (73). From this point of view, the christological character of the Beatitudes is clear. "The disciple is bound to the mystery of Christ. His life is immersed in communion with Christ: 'It is no longer I who live, but Christ who lives in me' (Gal 2:20). The Beatitudes are the transposition of the Cross and Resurrection into discipleship. But they apply to the disciple because they were first paradigmatically lived by Christ himself" (74).

This becomes even more apparent, according to Ratzinger, in the Beatitudes-portion of Matt 5:3–12:

> Anyone who reads Matthew's text attentively will realize that the Beatitudes present a sort of veiled autobiography of Jesus, a kind of portrait of his figure. He who has no place to lay his head (cf. Mt 8:20) is truly poor; he who can say, "Come to me . . . for I am meek and lowly in heart" (cf. Mt 11:28–29) is truly meek; he is the one who is pure of heart and so unceasingly beholds God. He is the peacemaker, he is the one who suffers for God's sake. The Beatitudes display the mystery of Christ himself, and they call us into communion with him. (74)

Ratzinger ignores the curious discrepancy between the wording of the first beatitude in Matthew—"the poor in spirit" (Matt 5:3) and in Luke—"the poor" (Luke 6:20). His motive for this is not made explicit, yet his book does have a theological purpose, which he serves by picking and choosing what to comment upon. Indeed, for Ratzinger, the historicity of the two passages, with their respective contexts, is less important than the theological position reflected in Matthew, who, linking Old to

New, "remains completely in the tradition of the piety reflected in the Psalms and so in the vision of the true Israel expressed in them" (76). He follows this with a brief excursus on the history of interpretation of the first Beatitude, pointing to Francis of Assisi as its "most intensely lived illustration", and one who confirms Ratzinger's overall view: "The Saints are the true interpreters of Holy Scripture" (78).

Bypassing the second Beatitude for the moment, he proceeds to the third: "Blessed are the meek, for they shall inherit the earth" (Matt 5:5). After a survey of the Hebrew Bible's repeated promises of land since the time of Abraham (80–84), Ratzinger concludes by saying, "The earth ultimately belongs to the meek, to the peaceful, the Lord tells us. It is meant to become the 'land of the king of peace.' The third Beatitude invites us to orient our lives toward this goal" (84). This image of course has an application for the present:

> Every eucharistic assembly is for us Christians a place where the king of peace reigns in this sense. The universal communion of Christ's Church is thus a preliminary sketch of the world of tomorrow, which is destined to become a land of Jesus Christ's peace. In this respect, too, the third Beatitude harmonizes closely with the first: It goes some way toward explaining what 'Kingdom of God' means, even though the claim behind this term extends beyond the promise of the land. (84)

These remarks anticipate the seventh Beatitude: "Blessed are the peacemakers, for they shall be called sons of God" (Matt 5:9). Ratzinger relates this Beatitude to King Solomon, whose name derives from *shalom*, the Hebrew word for peace. According to 1 Chr 22:9–10, God had promised to be a father to Solomon; and he states a parallel with God and Jesus. "This brings to the fore a connection between divine Sonship and the kingship of peace: Jesus is the Son, and he is truly Son. He is therefore the true 'Solomon'—the bringer of peace. Establishing peace is part of the very essence of Sonship. The seventh Beatitude thus invites us to be and do what the Son does, so that we ourselves may become 'sons of God'" (85).

Now Ratzinger returns to the second Beatitude—"Blessed are those who mourn, for they shall be comforted"—with highly subjective if not poetic interpretations: There are two types of grieving. Judas Iscariot is a representative of the first kind; he gave up all hope and committed suicide. "Peter is an example of the second kind: Struck by the Lord's gaze, he bursts into healing tears that plow up the soil of his soul" (86).

After enumerating further examples of this latter kind of mourning, Ratzinger concludes:

> At the foot of Jesus' Cross we understand better than anywhere else what it means to say "blessed are those who mourn, for they shall be

comforted." Those who do not harden their hearts to the pain and need of others, who do not give evil entry into their souls, but suffer under its power and so acknowledge the truth of God—they are the ones who open the windows of the world to let the light in. It is to those who mourn in this sense that great consolation is promised. The second Beatitude is thus intimately connected with the eighth: "Blessed are those who are persecuted for righteousness' sake, for theirs is the kingdom of heaven (Mt 5:10)." (87)

This eighth Beatitude, for Ratzinger, "had a prophetic significance for Matthew and his audience. For them this was the Lord foretelling the situation of the Church which they were living through" (88). At the same time, the "crucified Christ is the persecuted just man portrayed in the words of Old Covenant prophecy—particularly the Suffering Servant Songs—but also prefigured in Plato's writings (*The Republic*, II 316e–362a). And in this guise he himself is the advent of God's Kingdom. This Beatitude is an invitation to follow the crucified Christ—an invitation to the individual as well as to the church as a whole" (89).[4]

The final Beatitude—"Blessed are you, when [people] revile you and persecute you . . . for my sake "—presents the person of Jesus, and the believer's commitment to him, as decisive for salvation. "In the other Beatitudes, Christology is present, so to speak, in veiled form; here, however, the message that he himself is the center of history emerges openly. Jesus ascribes to his 'I' a normative status that no teacher of Israel—indeed no teacher of the Church—has a right to claim for himself. Someone who speaks like this is no longer a prophet in the traditional sense" (90). This clearly defined Christology thus becomes the ultimate foundation of the Sermon on the Mount altogether.

Returning now to the fourth Beatitude—"Blessed are those who hunger and thirst for righteousness, for they shall be satisfied"—Ratzinger interprets: "This saying is intrinsically related to Jesus' words concerning those who mourn and who will find comfort. In the earlier Beatitude the ones who receive the promise are those who do not bow to the diktat of prevailing opinions and customs, but resist it by suffering. Similarly, this Beatitude is concerned with those who are on the lookout, who are in search of something great, of true justice, of the true good" (90).

This exposition is followed by an excursus on "the salvation of those who do not know Christ" (92). Against what he sees as the prevailing view today, namely that "everyone should live by the religion—or perhaps by the atheism—in which he happens to find himself already" (92), Ratzinger launches the emphatic counsel: "No, God demands the opposite: that we become inwardly attentive to his quiet exhortation, which is present in us and which tears us away from what is merely habitual and puts us on the road of truth. To 'hunger and thirst for righteousness'—that is the path that lies open to everyone; that is the way that finds its destination in Jesus Christ" (92).

At last Ratzinger turns to the Beatitude thus far unmentioned: "Blessed are the pure in heart, for they shall see God" (Matt 5:8). Its words must, he says, be read primarily in the context of the Old Testament. Nonetheless, on Jesus' lips they "acquire new depth. For it belongs to his nature that he sees God, that he stands face-to-face with him, in permanent interior discourse—in a relation of Sonship. In other words, this Beatitude is profoundly Christological" (95).

A little later Ratzinger turns to the four proclamations of woe that follow the Beatitudes only in the Gospel of Luke (6:24–26). They assail those who are rich, well fed, merry, and highly regarded. His response is that these proclamations of woe "are not condemnations; they are not an expression of hatred, or of envy, or of hostility. The point is not condemnation, but a warning that is intended to save" (97). These warnings, as well as the Beatitudes in general, stand opposed to our spontaneous sense of existence and demand conversion in order to bring "what is pure and noble to the fore" (98).

Critique

On p. 70: Here and elsewhere Ratzinger regards Matt 5:17–18 as representing genuine—that is, historically valid—words of Jesus. Yet an informed analysis of the two verses and their immediate context reveals the passage as anything but genuine, as will be seen.

Matthew 5:17–20

The new righteousness

[17]Do not think that I have come to abolish the law or the prophets; I have not come to abolish but to fulfill. [18]For amen, I say to you, till heaven and earth pass away, neither the smallest stroke nor a dot of the law will pass away until all is fulfilled. [19]Whoever now relaxes one of the least of these commandments, and teaches people so [to do], will be called the least in the kingdom of heaven; but whoever follows and teaches (them) will be called great in the kingdom of heaven. [20]For I say to you: unless your righteousness far exceeds that of the scribes and Pharisees, you will not enter the kingdom of heaven.

Verse 17: This verse derives from Matthew in its entirety—that is, has no evident source in Mark or Q. The beginning corresponds to the introduction in Matt 10:34—also a purely Matthean phrase, and "fulfill" is one of his more frequently used words. In addition, the Matthean combination "law and prophets" is seen in 7:12 and 22:40.

Verse 18: The six words of introduction and the four concluding ones give the verse its Matthean character, but in all probability Q is the basis for the central part,[5] which puts emphasis on strict observance of the Torah. As we see also in the parallel phrase in Matt 24:34—the "until all has been fulfilled" of v 18 refers to the end of the world.

Verse 19: "The least of these commandments" is generally seen to refer to all of the teaching set forth by Jesus from 5:21 to 7:27.

Verse 20: This is a statement of principle. The word "for" implies a summary of the preceding words and at the same time introduces the warning that follows. The call to righteousness here attributed to Jesus measures itself antitypically by the caricature of the scribes and Pharisees, and demands good works and fruits (cf. 5:16).

In sum, Jesus of Nazareth did not utter any of the words contained in Matt 5:17–20. The whole passage is a Matthean composition except for v 18b–c, which reflects the formulation of an early Christian community that was committed to strict observance of the Jewish Law.

On p. 73: Ratzinger reads Paul's paradoxical feelings into the Beatitudes, and for him it therefore goes without saying that Paul was a disciple of Jesus. But Paul does not use the word "disciple" a single time in his letters. Moreover, Paul did not know Jesus personally, having "seen" him only through a mystical experience and in fact having avoided all contact with the direct disciples initially.[6] Therefore Ratzinger's facile syllogism is scarcely persuasive.

On pp. 70–99: Ratzinger uncritically accepts of the Beatitudes as genuine words of the historical Jesus. To demonstrate the falsity, if not naivety, of this assumption, I offer a brief analysis of the Beatitudes as they appear in both Matthew and Luke.

Matthew 5:1–12

The Beatitudes

[1]Now when he saw the multitudes, he went up the mountain, and when he sat down his disciples came to him. [2]And he opened his mouth, taught them and said:

[3]"Blessed are the poor in spirit; for theirs is the kingdom of heaven.
[4]Blessed are the sorrowful, for they shall be comforted.
[5]Blessed are the meek, for they shall inherit the earth.
[6]Blessed are they who hunger and thirst for righteousness
for they shall be filled.
[7]Blessed are the merciful, for they shall obtain mercy.
[8]Blessed are the pure in heart, for they shall see God.
[9]Blessed are the peacemakers, for they shall be called sons of God

¹⁰Blessed are they who are persecuted for righteousness' sake
for theirs is the kingdom of heaven.
¹¹Blessed are *you* when men revile you and persecute you and utter all kinds of evil against you falsely for my sake. ¹²Rejoice and be jubilant; for your reward will be great in heaven. For so did they persecute the prophets before you."

Luke 6:20–23

The Beatitudes

²⁰And he lifted up his eyes on his disciples, and said:

"Blessed are you poor, for yours is the kingdom of God.
²¹Blessed are you that hunger now, for you shall be satisfied.
Blessed are you that weep now, for you shall laugh.
²²Blessed are you when men hate you, and when they exclude you (from community) and revile you, and bring your name into disrepute because of the Son of Man. ²³Rejoice in that day, and dance for joy, for look, your reward is great in heaven; for so your fathers did to the prophets."

Luke 6:20b–23 finds its source-material in Q, as does Matt 5:3–12, but within the Lukan passages, we observe differences in sentence-construction between verses 20–21 and 22–23 The formal contrast needs to be considered here. Verses 20b and 21 can be dated as the earliest of the Beatitudes; significantly, they do not contain any reference to Jesus. More will be said on this presently.

Verses 22 and 23, on the other hand, presuppose the identity of Jesus as the Son of Man. They are specific to a particular situation and connect the persecution of Jesus' followers with the previous persecutions of the Old Testament prophets. A similar view is presented in 1 Thess 2:14–16 and Mark 12:1–12. In short, these verses reflect the post-Easter experiences of early Christian communities, and are thus clearly a later insertion.

To return to the earlier, original Beatitudes (vv 20b and 21), poverty, hunger and suffering are not listed as "blessings" but rather as examples of that which God will change, in accordance with the royal ideal known from tradition in Ps 72:4, 12–13:

⁴The king will judge the people with righteousness
and the poor with justice and crush the oppressor . . .
¹²He will deliver the poor who cries for help,
and the wretched who has no helper.
¹³He will be gracious to the little ones and the poor,
and the poor he will help.

The promise of the coming kingdom from the earliest Beatitude-source—Q—makes sense only if distress will be transformed in the near future. And the promise is tied up with expectation of a heavenly banquet.

The following historical conclusions can be drawn. First, the oldest section of the Beatitudes (Luke 6:20b–21) can be attributed to Jesus; for by contrast, the much longer series of ten blessings in Matt 5:3–12, shows signs of growth within the tradition. Second, the later sections—Luke 6:22–23/Matt 5:11–12—are focused on the situation of the post-Easter community.

As alluded to above, it is worth repeating that the often discussed difference between poverty and poverty of spirit can be clarified quite helpfully when one considers the historical context of the different Gospels. That is, the spiritualization of the Beatitudes in Matthew reflects the sense, in the earliest community, that concrete material promises of Jesus would be interpreted as radical and even offensive—thus dangerous for the community. In addition, of course, it was becoming increasingly necessary for Christians to accept that the coming of the kingdom of God, which was finally to bring about these promised changes, had been delayed.

In sum, Ratzinger's christological interpretation of the Beatitudes presumes that one and the same person pronounced all of them. This denies the historical layers of tradition and context. It also overlooks the fact that the earliest layer of the beatitudes has no shred of christological (or eschatological) content at all. In effect, Ratzinger is casting a piece of historical evidence in a mythological frame while insisting that his approach is scientific. Such a blatant inconsistency is not helpful either to scholarship or to the faith.

Overview of pp. 99–127
The Torah of the Messiah

This section is divided into four parts: 1) "You Have Heard That It Was Said . . . But I Say To You" (99–106); 2) "The Dispute Concerning the Sabbath" (106–112); 3) "The Fourth Commandment: The Family, the People, and the Community of Jesus' Disciples" (112–22); and 4) "Compromise and Prophetic Radicalism" (122–27).

1. According to the Judaic tradition, Ratzinger informs us, "the Messiah was expected to bring a renewed Torah—*his* Torah" (99). This finds its echo in the Sermon on the Mount, where "Jesus speaks to his people, to Israel, as to the first bearers of the promise" (101). Jesus' words in Matt 5:17–20 (see above, pp. 48–49) are an "interpretative key" for the Sermon on the Mount making "God's fidelity to himself and Jesus' fidelity to the faith of Israel unmistakably clear. . . . The intention

is not to abolish, but to fulfill, and this fulfillment demands a surplus, not a deficit, of righteousness" (101–2). Moreover, one cannot but be stunned "by Jesus' presentation of the relationship of Moses' Torah to the Torah of the Messiah in a series of antitheses: 'It was said to them of old . . . but I say to you. . . .' Jesus' 'I' is accorded a status that no teacher of the Law can legitimately allow himself" (102). Such an assertion on Jesus' part is obviously triggered by "the open claim that he himself is on the same exalted level as the Lawgiver—as God" (102). The amazement of the people at Jesus' words (Matt 7:28) "is precisely over the fact that a human being dares to speak with the authority of God. Either he is misappropriating God's majesty—which would be terrible—or else, and this seems almost inconceivable, he really does stand on the same exalted level as God " (102–3).

Ratzinger now reports that much of his own thinking on the Sermon on the Mount was inspired by Jacob Neusner's *A Rabbi Talks with Jesus*. In his book Neusner joins Jesus' many disciples on the "mount" in Galilee and listens to Jesus, during which he became aware of the centrality of the "I" in Jesus' message—an element that gave everything a new direction (105). Agreeing with Neusner, and noting by way of example Jesus' injunction to the rich young man to "sell all you have and come and follow *me*" (Matt 19:20), Ratzinger concludes that "the state of being holy as God is holy (cf. Lev 19:2; 11:44), as demanded by the Torah, now consists in following Jesus" (105).

2. Concerning the dispute over the Sabbath, Ratzinger points to Neusner's comments on Matt 12:5–8. When in v 6 "Jesus says that something greater than the Temple is here," according to Neusner-Ratzinger, "he can only mean that he and his disciples may do on the Sabbath what they do because they stand in the place of the priests in the Temple: the holy place has shifted, now being formed by the circle made up of the master and his disciples."[7]

For Neusner, "rest" is an essential element of the Sabbath and the inner link to Jesus' exulting exclamation, "I thank thee, Father, Lord of heaven and earth, that though hast hidden these things from the wise and understanding and revealed them to babes" (Matt 11:25). These two texts show, Ratzinger proposes, that the dispute over the Sabbath and the divinity of Jesus are closely related, "for in both cases the issue is the mystery of Jesus—the 'Son of Man,' the 'Son' par excellence" (109).

The keyword "rest" constitutes a continuing thread in the praising of God by Jesus, as we see in Matt 11:28–30: "Come to me, all who labor and are heavy laden, and I will give you rest. Take my yoke upon you, and learn from me; for I am gentle and lowly in heart, and you will find rest for your souls. For my yoke is easy, and my burden is light." Neusner—again supported by Ratzinger—summarizes the content thus: "[M]y yoke is easy, I give you rest, the son of man is lord of the Sabbath indeed, because the son of man is now Israel's Sabbath: how we act like God."⁸

Thus, we are told, the dispute over the Sabbath has been resolved: "Jesus understands himself as the Torah—as the word of God in person. The tremendous prologue of John's Gospel—'in the beginning was the Word, and the Word was with God, and the Word was God' (Jn 1:1)—says nothing different from what the Jesus of the Sermon on the Mount and the Jesus of the Synoptic Gospels says. The Jesus of the Fourth Gospel and the Jesus of the Synoptics is [sic] one and the same; the true 'historical' Jesus" (110–11). (Ratzinger clearly has no trouble assigning historical reality to an abstract entity—the Jesus of faith—this despite the premise of his book and the years of responsible scholarly training that should have laid sufficient foundation for a more sensible exposition.}

3. Ratzinger summarizes Neusner's contention with Jesus concerning the fourth commandment—to honor father and mother. For Neusner, Jesus' teaching in Matt 12:46–50 menaces the family of Israel, "and the foundations of Israel's social order are thrust aside by the primacy of his person" (113). A little later Ratzinger writes: "Discipleship of Jesus offers no politically concrete program for structuring society. . . . This restructuring of the social order finds its basis and its justification in Jesus' claim that he, with his community of disciples, forms the origin and center of a new Israel. Once again we stand before the 'I' of Jesus, who speaks on the same level as the Torah itself, on the same level as God" (114). Whereupon Rabbi Neusner concludes, "I now realize, only God can demand of me what Jesus is asking."⁹ Ratzinger arrives at a similar conclusion: "If Jesus is God, then he is entitled and able to handle the Torah as he does" (115).

Confronted with the question of whether Jesus was justified in founding a community that undermined the social order of Israel, Ratzinger points out that "Israel does not exist simply for itself, in order to live according to the 'eternal' dispositions of the Law—it exists to be a light to the nations" (116). Furthermore, there is the promise "that the boundaries will fall and that the God of Israel will be acknowledged and revered by all the nations as their God, as the one God" (116). This in fact is what Jesus accomplished. "He has brought the God of Israel to the nations. . . . He has brought the gift of universality, which was the one great definitive promise to Israel and the world" (116).

One consequence of this is:

> "This universalization of Israel's faith and hope, and the concomitant liberation from the letter of the Law for the new communion with Jesus, is tied to Jesus' authority and his claim to Sonship. It loses

its historical weight and its whole foundation if Jesus is interpreted merely as a liberal reform rabbi.... The leap into universality, the new freedom that such a leap requires, is possible only on the basis of a greater obedience. Its power to shape history can come into play only if the authority of the new interpretation is no less than the authority of the original: It must be a divine authority."[10] (119–20)

4. After lengthy discussions of casuistic and apodictic law[11] in the Old Testament (123–25) Ratzinger concludes that "Jesus does nothing new or unprecedented when he contrasts the practical, casuistic norms developed in the Torah with the pure will of God, which he presents as 'the greater righteousness'" (126) (cf. Matt 5:20). As the chosen prophet Jesus "takes up the intrinsic dynamism of the Torah itself, as further developed by the Prophets, and ... he gives it its radical form" (126). Indeed, Jesus fulfills the Torah "by assigning reason its sphere of responsibility for acting within history" (126).

Critique

On p. 99: For a critique of the Messiah's bringing a renewed or personal Torah, see above, p. 44.

On p. 101: In the Sermon on the Mount, the historical Jesus is *not* "speaking to his own people, to Israel." As has been discussed above, it is a compilation of diverse elements arranged by the evangelist Matthew; Jesus delivered no such oration—on a hill or anywhere else. Furthermore, the text has Jesus eluding the crowd by climbing the mountain, whereupon he directed his words to the disciples (5:1–2). Yet according to 7:28 the whole sermon was directed at the crowd referred to in 5:1a.

On p. 102: The antitheses in Matt 5:21–48[12]—the series of emphatic statements beginning with "but I say to you"—follow the rhetorical pattern of argumentation of Jewish law-teachers instructing in the method of countering differences of opinion. In this section, Jesus is unique in his adopting this pattern to refute requirements of the law.[13] It is of course probable that some Jews objected, considering this as invading the sphere of God. But there is nothing to suggest that invoking antitheses amounts to a claim to be on the same level as God. Besides, the content of these antitheses (with the possible exception of the prohibition against oaths) was routinely taught by contemporary Jews.

On pp. 105–27: It appears that in his apologetic interests, Ratzinger has misappropriated ideas from Neusner's popular book. Regarding Neusner's picture of Jesus—one who acts like God—as a historical representation, Ratzinger presumes to incorporate this into his own "historical" reconstruction. It must be said, however, that this runs directly counter to what Neusner wrote. In the latter's use of the solely "Jewish" Gospel, Matthew, Neusner's explicit intention was to enter into dialogue with the Jesus of the first gospel because "Matthew's picture of Jesus describes him as a Jew among Jews, unlike the portrait, for instance, given by John, who speaks of the 'Jews' with hatred."[14] Neusner's observations on the texts from Matthew and their contexts are for personal if not pastoral use;[15] and they ought not to be used to support statements about the historical Jesus, which is what Ratzinger does repeatedly.[16] What is more, Ratzinger has overlooked Neusner's strict caveat in this regard: "I make no claim whatsoever about the historical veracity of what Matthew says Jesus said and did. That is an issue confronting scholars."[17] He is to be lauded for his open admission, for at least the reader knows where he stands; this is not the case with Ratzinger, who continually crosses the line between apologetics and historical interests. What results, of course, is anything but scholarly.

On pp. 109–11: Matt 11:25–30 does not justify the claim that Jesus considered himself as the Torah; for Jesus himself did not utter the words of this passage. This will become clear from the analysis below.

Matthew 11:25–30
Jesus' Praise and the Comfortable Words
[25]I praise you, Father, Lord of heaven and earth, because you have hidden this from the wise and understanding and revealed it to babes. [26]Yes, Father, for this was your gracious will. [27]All things have been given to me by my Father, and no one knows the Son except the Father, and no one knows the Father except the Son, andthe one whom the Son chooses to reveal it. [28]Come to me all who labor and are heavy-laden, and I will give you rest. [29]Take my yoke on you and learn from me, for I am gentle and lowly in heart, and you will find rest for your souls. [30]For my yoke is easy and my burden is light.

Verses 25–27 come from Q (see as well Luke 10:21–22). Jesus' activity is expressed in the customary style of the revelation-discourse. The words are not authentic, and presuppose the Easter-event. Cf. the words of the "risen" Jesus in Matt 28:18 ("All authority . . . has been given to me") with v 27a ("All things have been given to me").

Verses 28–30 are known as the "Comfortable Words." They have countless parallels in Wisdom literature—see only Prov 8:1–21. "Gentle" and "lowly" have an ethical significance in Matthew (5:5, 7; 21:5); that is, they stress the need to behave gently and in a lowly way. Although the expression may be taken in a generic sense, it is not unlikely that "the weary and heavy laden" here refer to the actual audience, that it, those burdened by Pharisaic demands (cf. 23:4). Verses 28–30 could not be authentic sayings of Jesus, for they presume his equation with personified Wisdom, which only arose in the post-Easter context, when Christians transferred to their Lord—the capital letter has the same effect here—what in pre-Christian times Jews had said about Wisdom. In essence, this equation corresponds that of Jesus with the Word (in Greek, *logos*) in John 1:1: "In the beginning was the Word, and the Word was with God, and the Word was God." That is, these are later christological formulations, similar to those in Matt 11:28–30, and cannot in any way be traced to the historical Jesus of Nazareth.

> **THE BOTTOM LINE:** Jesus' reinterpretation of the Torah in the Sermon on the Mount in no way implies a claim on his part to be equal to God. Even Matthew is careful to show the Son's subordination to the Father.

Chapter Seven
on Chapter 5
The Lord's Prayer

Since the gospels portray the Lord's Prayer as one intended for recitation by Jesus' Jewish followers, Ratzinger's Christian interpretation cannot represent its original meaning.

Overview

By way of introduction, Ratzinger explains why the Lord's Prayer is part of the Sermon on the Mount: "If being human is essentially about relation to God, it is clear that speaking with, and listening to, God is an essential part of it. This is why the Sermon on the Mount also includes a teaching about prayer. The Lord tells us how to pray" (128).

Matt 6:5–8 introduces the prayer itself "by a short catechesis on prayer. Its main purpose is to warn against false forms of prayer" such as "showing off before others" (128).

After detailed discussions about prayer in general (130–32), Ratzinger correctly remarks that "Luke places the Our Father in the context of Jesus' own praying" (132), for he was at prayer when one of the disciples asked him to teach them how to pray (Luke 11:1). Ratzinger's subsequent observations about Luke's contextualization of the prayer claim to explain both the historical Jesus and the gospel-writer's interpretation of the prayer: "Jesus thereby involves us in his own prayer; he leads us into the interior prayer; he leads us into the interior dialogue of triune love; he draws our human hardship deep into God's heart, as it were" (132). It is therefore not surprising that in his subsequent interpretation, Ratzinger tells us to remember that it originates in Jesus' "own praying, from the Son's dialogue with the Father" (133).

As to the two different versions of the prayer, Ratzinger says only that "[t]he Our Father has been transmitted to us in a shorter form in Luke, whereas it comes down to us in Matthew in the version that the Church has adopted for purposes of prayer. The discussion about which is more original is not superfluous, but neither is it the main issue"

(133). The seven petitions in Matthew plainly make known "things that Luke seems in part only to touch upon" (134).

Before beginning his exposition, Ratzinger explains the structure of the Our Father in Matthew. "It comprises an initial salutation and seven petitions. Three are 'thou-petitions,' while four are 'we-petitions.' The first three petitions concern the cause of God himself in this world; the four following petitions concern our hopes, needs, and hardships" (134). We must remember, he urges, that the Our Father is at all times a prayer of Jesus, and that communion with him is what opens its meaning to us: "We pray to the Father in heaven, whom we know through his Son. And that means that Jesus is always in the background during the petitions. . . . A final point—because the Our Father is a prayer of Jesus, it is a Trinitarian prayer: We pray with Christ through the Holy Spirit to the Father" (135).

Following these introductory remarks, Ratzinger presents what he a more detailed exposition of the prayer.

Our: This word, Ratzinger informs us, represents a challenge. "It requires that we step out of the closed circle of our 'I.' It requires that we surrender ourselves to communion with the other children of God. . . . In this sense, the Our Father is at once a fully personal and a thoroughly ecclesial prayer" (141).

Father: According to Jesus "there are two sides of God's Fatherhood for us to see" (137). For one thing, God, as our creator, is our Father. For another, "Jesus is 'the Son' in the strict sense—he is of one substance with the Father. He wants to draw all of us into his humanity and so into his Sonship, into his total belonging to God" (138). God is not, however, also our mother and is never addressed as such; so that even if maternal love is part of God's image in the Bible (cf. Isa 66:13; 49:15), and if we have other ideas according to our personal or societal concerns, we must remember that "the prayer language of the entire Bible remains normative for us, in which, as we have seen, while there are some fine images of maternal love, 'mother' is not used as a title or a form of address for God. We make our petitions in the way that Jesus, with Holy Scripture in the background, taught us to pray, and not as we happen to think or want. Only thus do we pray properly" (140).

Who art in heaven: These words give evidence for the truth that, "while we have different earthly fathers, we all come from one single Father. . . . Heaven, then, means that other divine summit from which we all come and to which we are all meant to return. The fatherhood that is 'in heaven' points us toward the greater 'we' that transcends all boundaries, breaks down all walls, and creates peace" (141–42).

Hallowed be thy Name: The first petition recalls the Commandment not to take the name of God in vain (Exod 20:7). "But what is this 'name of God'?" (142) asks Ratzinger. For when Moses asked this, he received only a cryptic answer: "I am who I am" (Exod 3:14). "This pledge is a name and a non-name at the same time" (143). Nevertheless, it does have a positive meaning. "What began at the burning bush in the Sinai desert comes to fulfillment at the burning bush of the Cross. God has now truly made himself accessible in his incarnate Son. He has become part of our world; he has, as it were, put himself into our hands" (144). And thus the second petition of the Our Father becomes better understandable. "The more he gives himself into our hands, the more we can obscure his light" (144). Therefore the petition asks "that he himself take charge of the sanctification of his name" (144).

Thy Kingdom come: When in 1 Kgs 3:9 God promises to grant Solomon one request, the wise king asks for understanding—or, as Ratzinger renders it, a "listening heart." Jesus, he says, wants to direct us in this same way: "The first and essential thing is a listening heart, so that God, not we, may reign. The Kingdom of God comes by way of a listening heart" (146). As is frequently the case with Ratzinger, he offers by way of conclusion an imprecise syllogism: since "Jesus is the Kingdom of God in person, . . . the request for a listening heart becomes a request for communion with Jesus Christ" and ultimately "makes us one body with him" (146–47).[1]

Thy will be done on earth as it is in heaven: Two things follow from this petition, we are told. One is that "God has a will with and for us" that must become "the measure of our willing and being." The other is that heaven is "where God's will is unswervingly done. Or, to put in somewhat different terms, where God's will is done is heaven" (147).

Expanding on the first point, Ratzinger asks what God's will might in fact be. The answer he provides for the reader is that according to biblical presuppositions, human beings ultimately have a knowledge of God's will, but it is "covered over in many ways, like a barely flickering flame, all too often at risk of being smothered under the ash of all the prejudices that have piled up within us. And that is why God has spoken to us anew, uttering words in history that come to us from outside and complete the interior knowledge that has become all too hidden" (148). At the core of this "historical" teaching are the Ten Commandments, which by no means have been abolished by the Sermon on the Mount, but rather "developed further in a way that allows its full depth and grandeur to shine forth in all its purity" (148).

Turning to the second point, Ratzinger argues on the basis of biblical passages[2] "that Jesus himself is 'heaven' in the deepest and truest sense of the word—he in whom and through whom God's will is wholly done" (150). The third petition of the Our Father is therefore a request "that we come closer and closer to him, so that God's will can conquer the downward pull of our selfishness and make us capable of the lofty height to which we are called" (150).

Give us this day our daily bread: Jesus invites us "to pray for our food and thus to turn our care over to God" (150). Since in this context Jesus speaks of "our" bread, it is inappropriate for an individual to think of himself or herself alone. Furthermore, one should note that this petition "presupposes that the community of his closest disciples followed the Lord in a radical way, renouncing worldly possessions" (153).

The "daily" bread can be interpreted both in terms of what we need to live today—"what is necessary for existence"—and what we will need in the days or the time to come: "for the future, for the following day." But Ratzinger does not allow this conception of the future to remain on the literal level. In fact, he uses this occasion to expatiate on a complex theological point, thus wandering quite far from the simple words of the prayer:

> But the petition to receive tomorrow's bread today does not seem to make sense when looked at in the light of the disciples' existence. The reference to the future would make more sense if the object of the petition were the bread that really does belong to the future: the true manna of God. In that case, it would be an eschatological petition, the petition for an anticipation of the world to come, asking the Lord to give already "today" the future bread, the bread of the new world—himself. (154)

And next he retreats somewhat from the abstruse to the more general theological interpretation—that is, to the larger context of Jesus' words and actions. "The theme of bread has an important place in Jesus message—from the temptation in the desert and the multiplication of the loaves right up to the Last Supper" (155). He carries this line of reasoning so far as to insist that in the eucharistic sacrament, Jesus' " 'becoming-corporeal' is actually the real 'becoming-spiritual,'" and to discover in John 6—the speech on the bread of life—the full sweep of this theme. And he caps off his peroration with the claim: "When we consider Jesus' message in its entirety, then it is impossible to expunge the eucharistic dimension from the fourth petition of the Our Father" (156). Such an insight, however deeply felt, is not the product of historical reasoning, and has no place in a treatise that claims to be scholarly. In fact, it is a Monday morning analysis of a Sunday's game.

And forgive us our trespasses, as we forgive those who trespass against us: How to overcome guilt "is a central question for every human life" (157). Forgiveness is in fact a topic that permeates the Gospel of Matthew, from Jesus' call for reconciliation in 5:23–24, to his kneeling "before his disciples and wash[ing] their dirty feet, cleansing them with his humble love" (158). He asserts that "at its deepest core, [this request] is—like the other petitions—a Christological prayer. It reminds us of him who allowed forgiveness to cost him descent into the hardship of human existence and death on the Cross. It calls us first and foremost to thankfulness for that, and then, with him, to work through and suffer through evil by means of love" (160).

And lead us not into temptation: For some this petition is in fact theologically difficult—even shocking—for according to Jas 1:13, God does not lead people into temptation. Ratzinger finds a solution for this paradox in the parallel seen in the book of Job. "God gives Satan the freedom to test Job, though within precisely defined boundaries; God does not abandon man, but he does allow him to be tried" (162). Ratzinger offers the analogy: "Just as the juice of the grape has to ferment in order to become a fine wine, so too man needs purifications and transformations; they are dangerous for him, . . . and yet they are indispensable as paths on which he comes to himself and to God" (162).

But deliver us from evil: Ratzinger proposes not only that this petition gives the previous one "a positive twist" (164), but also that it "brings us back to the first three: In asking to be liberated from the power of evil, we are ultimately asking for God's Kingdom, for union with his will, and for the sanctification of his name" (167).

Critique

It is quite extraordinary that in a book claiming to contain an objective analysis of Jesus' life and teaching, Ratzinger does not discuss the composite nature of the Lord's Prayer, nor mention the curious fact that it is absent from both Mark and John. It is of course the case that, derived from Q (which he does not mention), and presented in two different versions, this double-indemnification must lead to the conclusion that it was not spoken by the historical Jesus. The closest Ratzinger comes to a substantive comment on this is in his superficial (pastoral) assurance that the noticeably different Matthean and Lukan versions both contain "thoughts Jesus wished to pass on to us" (133). The opportunity for scholarly exegesis has been ignored once again.

On p. 138: The text does not state—or even imply—that Jesus is "of one substance with the Father." This arbitrary choice of dogma by Ratzinger in fact reveals a dismissal of the social-historical upheaval lying behind the creedal formula—not to mention that the sentiment was formally adopted some 300 years after the "Easter-event." Such a sophisticated concept is far from exegetically acceptable in this context.

On pp. 146–47: In his petition for the advent of the kingdom of God, Jesus does not refer to himself as the Kingdom personified. The "kingdom of God" — meaning "God's imperial rule" — is for all intents and purposes a new coinage. That is, Jesus has replaced the traditional concept of God's reaching into history, seen in such passages as Isa 35:4: "Say to those who are of a fearful heart: 'Be strong, fear not! Look, your God will come with vengeance, with the recompense of God. He will come and save you.'" Thus Jesus has inaugurated a new concept, which was later translated into the primitive Christian expectation of the return of Jesus as Lord (cf. 1 Cor 11:26; 16:22). Therefore the second petition of the Our Father cannot be derived from the earliest communities. It goes back to the historical Jesus, who prays for the coming of the Kingdom of God.

On pp. 155–56: The petition for bread neither refers to nor even implies the Eucharist, but has in mind the need of the destitute for daily sustenance. Having neither homes nor regular income, Jesus and his followers were of course dependent on daily donations.[3]

On p. 158: Once again Ratzinger harmonizes the different Gospel reports. He claims that prior to the Eucharist Jesus washed the disciples' feet. But in the gospel under discussion here, that of Matthew, he does not wash their feet; and while it is true that John narrates a foot-washing (chapter 13), he does not report anything similar to a eucharistic event, but merely a regular meal. Ratzinger is thus reading the eucharist passages of the Synoptics — which have no foot-washing accounts — into the Johannine account. Once again he has disregarded historical authenticity. And in this case the result is ironic, for in accepting the authenticity of conflicting accounts, he effectively undermines all chance that either could be regarded historically.

On p. 162: By invoking a real existence and moral effectiveness of Satan, Ratzinger of course forsakes historical argument. The presupposition of mythical persons and events behind a purportedly responsible exegesis is almost too incredible to warrant comment; in technical terms it amounts to methodological nonsense.

> **THE BOTTOM LINE:** Ratzinger's ecclesial interpretation of the Our Father faces the fundamental and insurmountable obstacle that this prayer was intended to be appropriate and relevant for every Jew, not only for the members of the circle around Jesus. From an historical perspective, then, a christological understanding makes no sense.

Chapter Eight
on Chapter 6
The Disciples

> Ratzinger effectively disavows the gospel reports
> of Jesus' special powers, and thereby distorts the
> way both Jesus and his kingdom proclamation
> appeared to his contemporaries.

Overview

In this chapter Ratzinger wants simply to "listen to the most important texts that show the formation of the community of Jesus' closest disciples" (169). In this regard, for Ratzinger the basic text is Mark 3:13–19, the calling of the disciples on a mountain, i.e. the place of Jesus' communion with God. Their calling as a prayer-event is even more explicitly underscored in the Lucan parallel account (6:12–13). "The calling of the Twelve, far from being purely functional, takes a deeply theological meaning: Their calling emerges from the Son's dialogue with the Father and is anchored there" (170).

The phrase from Mark 3:14, "he 'made' twelve" [NRSV, 'appointed'], takes up "Old Testament terminology for appointment to the priesthood" (171) as 1 Kgs 12:31 and 13:33 show. Yet, the individual naming of the chosen ones indicates a prophetic dimension of their ministry. Besides, "the number twelve is a return to the origins of Israel, and yet at the same time it is a symbol of hope: The whole of Israel is restored and the twelve tribes are newly assembled" (171). Also, he says, twelve is a cosmic figure that indicates the universal inclusiveness of the People of God.

"This is also the right context for the prophecy in which Jesus gives Nathanael a glimpse of his true nature" (171). Cf. John 1:51: "You will see the heaven opened, and the angels of God ascending and descending upon the Son of man." From this "prophecy" Ratzinger derives the following conclusion:

> Jesus reveals himself here as the new Jacob. The patriarch dreamed
> that he saw a ladder set up beside his head, which reached up to

heaven and on which God's angels were ascending and descending. This dream has become a reality with Jesus. He himself is the 'gate of heaven' (Gen 28:10–22); he is the true Jacob, the 'Son of Man,' the patriarch of the definitive Israel." (172)

For one thing, the Twelve must be with Jesus "so as to be able to recognize his oneness with the Father" (172); for another, their job is to preach Jesus' message and to exorcise the powers of evil. "[T]he ancient world did in fact experience the birth of Christianity as a liberation from the fear of demons" (173). Paul's statement that there is only one God and one Lord, Jesus Christ (1 Cor 8:4–6) was crucial: "These words imply a great liberating power—the great exorcism that purifies the world" (174). Ratzinger adds: "Faith in the one God is the only thing that truly liberates the world and makes it 'rational.' When faith is absent, the world only *appears* to be more rational" (174).

In Eph 6:10–12, he says, Paul has described the "exorcistic" nature of Christianity.

> [10]"Finally, be strong in the Lord and in the strength of his might. [11]Put on the whole armor of God, that you may be able to stand against the wiles of the devil. [12]For we are not contending against flesh and blood, but against the principalities, against the powers, against the world rulers of this present darkness, against the spiritual hosts of wickedness in the heavenly places." (174) [RSV]

Ratzinger interprets this text in an all-embracing comment on our present situation: "Who could fail to see here a description of our world as well, in which the Christian is threatened by an anonymous atmosphere, by 'something in the air' that wants to make the faith ludicrous and absurd to him?" (175).

Then in a return to the theme of the gospels that touches on the spiritual gifts given to Jesus' followers, he points out that, in another such passage, this time Matt 10:1, the disciples are endowed with the power "to heal every disease and every infirmity." Yet he is quick to distinguish between spirituality and hocus-pocus; for their authority "to cast out demons . . . rules out any magical understanding of healing. . . . The healing power of the messengers of Jesus Christ is opposed to the spirits of magic; it exorcises the world in medical terms as well" (176). And as if concerned that the powers be given too weighty a position in the text, Ratzinger warns that the place of exorcism in the ministry of Jesus must be kept in its proper context.

> For Jesus himself and for his followers, miracles of healing are . . . an subordinate element within the overall range of his activity which is concerned with something deeper, with nothing less than the

'Kingdom of God': his becoming-Lord in us and in the world. Just as exorcism drives out the fear of demons and commits the world—which comes from God's reason—to our human reason, so, too, healing by God's power is both a summons to faith in God and a summons to use the powers of reason in the service of healing." (176–77)

The Twelve, he notes, were observant Jews who looked forward to the salvation of Israel; yet as individuals with their own personalities they were quite different. "This helps us to understand how difficult it was to initiate them gradually into Jesus' mysterious new way, of the kinds of tensions that had to be overcome" (178).

The sending out of a second group of 70 (or 72) disciples reported in Luke 10:1–12 likewise involves a symbolic number. "Based on a combination of Deuteronomy 32:8 and Exodus 1:5, seventy was considered to be the number of the nations of the world" (179). Thus the Seventy "are an intimation of the universal character of the Gospel, which is meant for all peoples of the earth" (180).

Among this broader group of "missionaries," then, Ratzinger implies that women would not only play a role but that in fact they have a demonstrably important place in the gospels, as loyal followers of Jesus (see Luke 8:1–3). He then proceeds to highlight other noteworthy features of Luke, who, in addition to stressing the women's presence, exhibits empathy for the poor as well as "a particular understanding for the Jews; the passions that were stirred up by the incipient separation between the Synagogue and the nascent Church—which left their traces in both Matthew and John—are nowhere to be found in [Luke]" (181). Indeed, he takes Luke 5:39[1] as a significant example of "understanding for those who wished to remain with the 'old wine'" (181). And he concludes his enumeration of Luke's textual qualities with his repeated stressing that Jesus' words and actions are rooted in prayer, arising as they do "from his inner oneness with the Father, from the dialogue between Father and Son" (182).

Ratzinger closes the chapter with a purportedly logical deduction: "If we have good reason to be convinced that the 'Holy Scriptures' are inspired, that they matured in a special sense under the guidance of the Holy Spirit, then we also have good reason to be convinced that precisely these specific aspects of the Lukan tradition preserve essential features of the original figure of Jesus for us" (182). The difficulty rests, however, with his attempt to build a "reasoned" conclusion on the basis of presupposed acceptance of divine inspiration that overrides historicity. It is an apple-and-oranges argument unworthy of his ascribed scholarship, to say the least.

Critique

On pp. 174–75: Ratzinger irresponsibly actualizes the biblical message by writing: "Faith in the one God is the only thing that truly liberates the world and makes it 'rational'. When faith is absent, the world only *appears* to be more rational." Indeed, his statement is commensurate with doctrine of his particular Catholic strain, but this in no way allows him to manipulate rationality per se in defense of his own Judeo-Christian God.

On pp. 176–77: Ratzinger plays down the miraculous elements of Jesus' ministry, preferring to let the irrational magic be "corrected" by means of doctrinally palatable analogy. The following brief analyses will be useful here.

Luke 10:18
I saw Satan fall like lightning from heaven.

The saying appears only in Luke, and constitutes Jesus' initial reaction to the return of the 70 disciples (Luke 10:1–12). Their mission had been highly successful, and they report that using his name had given them power over demons. The saying, however, seems misplaced, since Jesus' vision, although generally suited to a defeat of evil, does not clearly conform to the disciples' communication. That is, it would arguably be more fitting as Jesus' reaction to his own miraculous power. Nevertheless, the saying is unique and the only attestation of Jesus as a visionary. It is widely considered authentic, since it cannot be derived from primitive Christianity. That is, in the early church, victory over Satan was attributed to Jesus himself.[2] Moreover, it was generally assumed that Jesus had intimate contacts with the devil and with the demons subject to him, who recognized and feared who he was (cf. Mark 5:1–20; Luke 13:32). The Synoptic temptation-stories provide an often-overlooked legendary echo of this side of Jesus.[3]

Luke 11:20/Matthew 12:28
But if by the finger (in Matthew, *spirit*) of God I drive out demons, then the kingdom of God has come on you.

The logion comes from Q, and "finger of God" is certainly the original reading. For on the one hand, Matthew's version is governed by the context, in which mention of the spirit of God appears in both Matt 12:18 (=Isa 42:1) and 12:32. On the other hand, given the significance of the spirit in Luke-Acts, it is inconceivable that Luke would have changed a favorite motif to the somewhat unsettling image of "finger." "The finger of God" is undoubtedly an allusion to the miracles of Moses before the exodus from Egypt: the Egyptian magicians recognize the superiority of Moses with the words, "That is the finger of God" (Exod 8:15).

The historical Jesus' ministry foreshadows the fall of Satan, as his exorcisms make evident. The flight of the demons is a sign that the power of the evil one has been overcome, even if a final destruction of the evil powers will take place only at the final judgment.

As an additional illustration of a strong magical side of Jesus, consider the following story:

Mark 7:32–37

The deaf-mute

[32] And they brought him a deaf-mute and asked him to lay hands on him. [33] And he took him aside from the crowd of people and put his fingers in his ears, spat, and touched his tongue. [34] And looking up to heaven, he sighed and said to him, "*Ephphatha*," which means, "be opened." [35] And his ears were opened and immediately the fetter on his tongue was loosed and he spoke properly. [36] And he commanded them to tell no one. But the more he commanded them, the more they proclaimed it. [37] And they were astonished beyond measure and said: "He has done all things well; he makes even the deaf hear and the dumb speak."

In v 34 we find a magic word whose Greek translation[4]—as in other passages, cf. 1:44–45; 5:43a—derives from Mark. Verse 36 contains a motif of secrecy that is typical of that author[5]; by the similarly derived joyful exclamation of the crowd, the evangelist turns the single event into repeated occurrences. Note that the question of the identity of Jesus is also echoed here.[6]

The story contains a rich store of healing techniques: *first*, the manipulation, putting a finger in the ear; *second*, touching the tongue with spittle; *third*, the magic word (Ephphatha) which is necessary to free the tongue that is bound by a demonic spirit; and *fourth*, the segregation of the sick person. Indeed, the story reads almost like a list of instructions for Christian miracle workers.[7] A variant of the narrative appears later (8:22–26) without a magical word.

Concerning the historicity of the healing of a deaf-mute, a parallel may be drawn to the accounts of Jesus' healing of those possessed by demons. No doubt individual healings took place, but probably not with the frequency that the New Testament gospels suggest. Because of the number of specific details, however, the present narrative does have a high claim to authenticity. It shows the "magician" Jesus at work.

On p. 181: Ratzinger's thesis that, unlike the Gospels of Matthew and John, Luke demonstrates understanding or sensitivity toward the

Jews is incorrect. In fact, Luke paints them negatively, underlining their guilt in connection with Jesus' death, even to the point of having them responsible for his execution.[8] In this connection, Ratzinger also fails to consider Acts, for in chapters 2–5 of Luke's second book, the Jewish leaders are the opponents of the apostles, and in his missionary speeches Peter declares them responsible for Jesus' death.[9] In his first preaching, Paul boldly sets himself up in the Jews' synagogues, where he meets fierce opposition. Thereupon he turns to the Gentiles.[10] At the end of Acts, Paul cites Isaiah 6 against the Jews[11] who, contrary to the Gentiles, will not accept the message of salvation.[12] In sum, Luke has found the Jews both unreceptive and guilt-ridden—hardly the example of the "understanding" that Ratzinger is proposing.

On p. 182: Ratzinger claims that the doctrine of the divine inspiration of Scripture assures us that Jesus narratives found only in the Gospel of Luke have preserved essential features of the original figure of Jesus for us. This off-hand argument shows that he does not take historical-critical methodology at all seriously. His own "historical-critical method" neither questions nor even weighs the historical value of the gospels, for he is interested only in proclaiming their historicity.

> **THE BOTTOM LINE:** Ratzinger distorts the historical Jesus of Nazareth by playing down Jesus' magical powers which, after all, in his religious life were associated with the kingdom of God. He draws a bizarre line of demarcation between modern creative reasoning about God and early Christian exorcisms, suggesting in all seriousness that the latter were not stamped by magic. As always, the final arbiter of what constitutes truth is conformance to and usefulness in promoting speculative theological beliefs.

Chapter Nine
on Chapter 7
The Message of the Parables

By viewing the parables through the lens of an exalted Christ, Ratzinger overlooks their point and their power.

Having touched briefly on the parables in Chapter Three, Ratzinger now undertakes a more systematic treatment of the topic in two sections of Chapter Seven: "The Nature and Purpose of the Parables" and "Three Major Parables from the Gospel of Luke."

Overview of pp. 183–94
The Nature and Purpose of the Parables

The discourse begins with the following remarks: "There is no doubt that the parables constitute the heart of Jesus' preaching. While civilizations have come and gone, these stories continue to touch us anew with their freshness and humanity.... At the same time, though, we find ourselves in the same situation as Jesus' contemporaries and even his disciples: We need to ask him again and again what he wants to say to us in each of the parables (cf. Mk 4:10). The struggle to understand the parables correctly is ever present throughout the history of the Church. Even historical-critical exegesis has repeatedly had to correct itself and cannot give us any definite information" (183–84).

This is followed by a sketch of the new stage of research into the parables inaugurated by Adolf Jülicher (1857–1938), who underscored the fundamental difference between allegory and parable. Understanding an allegory requires discovering a single hidden meaning behind each individual element of a story. "Jülicher, for his part, sharply distinguished Jesus' parables from allegory; rather than allegory, he said, they are a piece of real life intended to communicate one idea, in the broadest possible sense—a single 'salient point'" (184–85).

Ratzinger agrees to the distinction between allegory and parable, but refuses to understand Jesus as simply the wisdom teacher presented by Jülicher (185–86). To reinforce this thesis he invokes the historical argument of Charles W. F. Smith:[1] "No one would crucify a teacher who told pleasant stories to enforce prudential morality." Indeed, Ratzinger concludes, "liberal exegesis . . . does not even come close to the real figure of Jesus" (186), the more so since it misses the eschatological and christological import of the parables.

Ratzinger recalls that, in his expositions of the Sermon on the Mount and the Lord's Prayer, "we have seen that the deepest theme of Jesus' preaching was his own mystery, the mystery of the Son in whom God is among us and keeps his word; he announces the Kingdom of God as coming and as having come in his person" (188). The same is true for the parables, Ratzinger says; and therefore he is able to agree with Joachim Jeremias, who concludes his book on the parables thus: "God's acceptable year has come. For he has been manifested whose veiled kingliness shines through every word and through every parable: the Savior" (188)[2].

While Ratzinger interprets "all the parables as hidden and multilayered invitations to faith in Jesus as the 'Kingdom of God in person, . . . there is one vexed saying of Jesus concerning the parables that stands in the way" (188). He is referring to the citation of Isa 6:9–10 by Mark 4:11–12. Ratzinger bases his reflection on the Jeremias' translation: "To you [that is to the circle of disciples] has been given the secret of the Kingdom of God: but to those who are without [read: "outside"], everything is obscure, in order that they (as it is written) may 'see and yet not see, may hear and yet not understand, unless they turn and God will forgive them'" (189)[3].

But it is through Isaiah that we will be able to understand these mysterious words of Jesus, Ratzinger claims. For, just as Jesus cites the prophet's words, we too,

> must read them in light of [Jesus'] own path, the outcome of which he already knows. In saying these words, Jesus places himself in the line of the Prophets—his destiny is a prophet's destiny. . . . Prophets fail: Their message goes too much against general opinion and the comfortable habits of life. It is only through failure that their word becomes efficacious. The failure of the Prophets is an obscure question mark hanging over the whole history of Israel, and in a certain way it constantly recurs in the history of humanity. Above all, it is also again and again the destiny of Jesus Christ: he ends up on the Cross. But that very Cross is the source of great fruitfulness. (189–90)

Whereupon Ratzinger raises the similar theme, present in John 12:24: "Truly, truly, I say to you, unless a grain of wheat falls into the earth and dies, it remains by itself alone; but if it dies, it bears much fruit."

He draws the conclusion that Jesus "himself is the grain of wheat. His 'failure' on the Cross is exactly the way leading from the few to the many, to all" (190), and adds Jesus' own conclusion from this same Gospel: "And I, when I am lifted up from the earth, will draw all to me" (John 12:32).

Thus this background of ultimate regeneration allows the failure of the prophets and of Jesus to acquire a positive meaning: "It is precisely the way to reach the point where 'they turn and God will forgive them.' It is precisely the method for opening the eyes and ears of all. It is on the Cross that the parables are unlocked" (190).

> The parables speak in a hidden way, then, of the Cross; they do not only speak of it—they are part of it themselves. For precisely because they allow the mystery of Jesus' divinity to be seen, they lead to contradiction. It is just when they emerge into a final clarity, as in the parable of the unjust vintners (Mk 12:1–12), that they become stations on the way to the Cross. In the parables Jesus is not only the sower who scatters the seed of God's word, but also the seed that falls into the earth in order to die and so to bear fruit. (191)

Jesus' troubling comment—in the echo of Isaiah—on the purpose of his parables in Mark 4:12, then, "is the very thing that leads us to their deepest meaning, provided—true to the nature of God's written word—we read the Bible, and especially the Gospels, as an overall unity expressing an intrinsically coherent message" (191).

Ratzinger concludes the section about the "Nature and the Purpose of the Parables" with the following remarks:

> [T]he parables are ultimately an expression of God's hiddenness in this world and of the fact that knowledge of God always lays claim to the whole person—that such knowledge is one with life itself, and that it cannot exist without 'repentance.' . . . In this sense, knowledge of God is possible only through the gift of God's love becoming visible, but this gift too has to be accepted. In this sense, the parables manifest the essence of Jesus' message. In this sense, the mystery of the Cross is inscribed right at the heart of the parables. (193–94)

Critique

On pp. 183–84: Ratzinger begins with a remark that distorts the discussion from the outset: "The struggle to understand the parables correctly is ever present throughout the history of the Church. Even historical-critical exegesis has repeatedly had to correct itself and cannot give us any definite information." As a former professor he should know that the scientific method never offers *final* solutions; nor is that its declared purpose.[4]

On p. 186: Ratzinger's citation of Charles W. F. Smith is in fact deceptive, for it is based on the false premise that Jesus was executed for telling pretty stories that advocated radical behavioral norms. If Jesus' parables led in any way to his execution, it was because they so often invoked the "kingdom of God"—God's imperial rule—and thus constituted a political threat to Rome. Furthermore, when Ratzinger claims that historical-critical criticism has not come close to the real figure of Jesus, he has neglected the fact that objective commentators have in fact demonstrated, if incompletely, a real, historical portrait of Jesus of Nazareth—one that, however, fails to support the idealized, exaggerated traditional paintings of a divine being, no matter how pious or imaginative.

On pp. 189–92: Ratzinger's citation of Mark 4:11–12 comes once again from Jeremias. Where this becomes problematic is that at the same time as he appropriates this scholar's translation, Ratzinger denies Jeremias his accompanying interpretation of the passage in question. That is, Jeremias in fact explicity rejects the use of Mark 4:11–12 as a canon to interpret Jesus' parables: "Hence we conclude that the logion is not concerned with the parables of Jesus."[5] This constitutes a half-reading of Jeremias in order to provide a bulwark for his own ideas on Mark's use of Isaiah. As a scholar, Ratzinger is displaying an unacceptable method of substantiation.

On p. 190: By way of refuting Ratzinger's repeated claim that the parables are "unlocked" on the Cross, that they speak of what he is pleased to call "the mystery of the Cross," let me first remind the reader of authentic parables of Jesus such as "The Dishonest Steward" (Luke 16:1–7) or "The Leaven" (Matt 13:33) that clearly do not allow a mystery-based interpretation.[6] Second, let me point to the non-authentic parable of the wicked tenants in Mark 12:1–11; it admittedly contains allusions to Jesus' death and therefore by extension to the cross, but it still cannot be used to support Ratzinger's claim, for it was composed by Christians who looked back on the death of Jesus and naturally enough employed references to his crucifixion.

For the sake of clarification I append a brief exegesis:

Mark 12:1–12

The wicked tenants

[1a]And he began to speak to them in parables:

[1b]"A man planted a vineyard, and set a hedge around it, and dug a pit for the wine press and built a tower, and let it out to tenants, and traveled to another country. [2]And he sent to the tenants at the appointed time a slave, so that he might receive from the tenants part of the fruits of the vineyard. [3]And they seized him, beat him and sent

him away (with) empty (hands). ⁴And again he sent to them another slave: him too they beat on the head and treated shamefully. ⁵And he sent another. They even killed that one, and many others, some they beat and others they killed.

⁶He still had one other, a beloved son. He sent him to them last, saying, 'They will respect my son.'

⁷Those tenants said to one another, 'This is the heir. Up, let us kill him and the inheritance will belong to us.' ⁸And they took him and killed him and flung his body out of the vineyard.

⁹What will the Lord of the vineyard do? He will come and destroy the tenants and give the vineyard to others.

¹⁰Do you not know this scripture [Ps 110:22–23], 'The stone which the builders have rejected, this has become the corner stone. ¹¹This has been done by the Lord and it is wonderful in our eyes'?"

¹²And they sought to seize him, for they knew that he had told the parable about them. But they feared the people, and so they left him and went away.

Verse 1a comes from "Mark." "In parables" (4:11) means "in a parabolic or cryptic manner." (Note that only a single parable follows.)

Verses 1b–11 have been adopted by Mark almost unchanged as a block of tradition, including the connecting formula, verse 10a, which was also present in the tradition (cf. 2:25 and 12:26). It is interesting that despite the considerable chronological and narrative distance from 9:7, Mark manages to span the gap with the expression "beloved son" (verse 6) and thus allusively reinscribes the legitimation of Jesus.

Verse 12 emphasizes who is being addressed in vv 1–11: the chief priests, scribes and elders from 11:27–28, against whom Jesus had told this story. Rather than the Jewish people, who prevented immediate action against Jesus and are portrayed approvingly in 11:32, it is the three groups of officials who represent the "unbelieving" Jews of the time of Mark. In further support of this, consider the corresponding accusation in 1 Thess 2:15, which similarly mentions the killing of the prophets and the killing of Jesus by the Jews. And above all recall Mark's passion account, in which the Jewish authorities lead the people astray, making them call for the death of Jesus (15:11–14).

Clearly, the text is an allegory based on the so-called "song of the vineyard" in Isa 5:1–7, and as such its true understanding depends on transferring all its essential elements to another frame of reference. Thus in the present text each of the main elements stands for something else:

- the vineyard (v 1) represents Israel;
- the tenants (v 1) are its leaders;
- the owner of the land (v 1) is God;
- the slaves (vv 2–5) are the prophets;

- the beloved son (v 6) is Christ;
- the killing of the son (v 8) refers to the murder of Jesus;
- the punishment of the tenants (v 9) stands for the rejection of Israel; and
- "the others" points to the Gentile Church.

The allegory, then, makes the following charge: since the Jewish leaders murdered Jesus, they themselves will be killed, and the true Israel, the Christian Church that superseded them, will be the Gentiles' justified inheritance. To substantiate this scripturally, then, Mark in vv 10–11 subsequently cites Ps 118:22–23. That is, the image used here, that of the *rejected* stone used God expressly as a central foundation, is a frequent proof-text in the early church for the resurrection of the rejected Christ.[7]

In sum, the parable of the wicked tenants can be properly understood only as an allegory composed for apologetic-narrative use by members of the early historical Christian community, that is as a thinly veiled "history" of what the actual community at the time was experiencing as opposed to a mysterious story told by Jesus à la Ratzinger.

Overview of pp. 194-201
The Good Samaritan
[Luke 10:25-37]

Luke presents this parable as Jesus' answer to a lawyer whom Jesus has told to love God and neighbor. The lawyer responds by asking for a definition of "neighbor." Ratzinger gives an outline of this parable, then describes its thrust: "The issue is no longer which other person is a neighbor to me or not. The question is about me. I have to become the neighbor, and when I do, the other person counts for me 'as myself'" (197).

Ratzinger subsequently applies the parable to the world at present, referring specifically to the peoples of Africa: "[W]e have given them the cynicism of a world without God" (198), while we ourselves are "surrounded by people who have been robbed and battered . . . victims of drugs, of human trafficking, of sex tourism" (199).

As a final interpretation, but upon quite another interpretive tack, Ratzinger offers that the Church Fathers in fact understood the parable christologically, and declares himself to be in their camp ultimately: "[W]hen we consider that in all the parables, each in a different way, the Lord really does want to invite us to faith in the Kingdom of God, which he himself is, then a Christological exposition is never a totally false reading" (199). He applies his christological lens to the figure of the half-dead man in the Samaritan-parable, and declares this betrodden character to be "an image of 'Adam,' of man in general" (199). Furthermore, "the road from Jerusalem to Jericho turns out to be an image of human history" (200), and "the Samaritan can only be the image of Jesus Christ" (200). And he rises above the historical to the universal in his overriding conclusion:

> We can safely ignore the individual details of the allegory, which change from Church Father to Church Father. But the great vision that sees man lying alienated and helpless by the roadside of history and God himself becoming man's neighbor in Jesus Christ is one that we can happily retain. . . . The two characters in this story are relevant to every single human being. Everyone is 'alienated,' especially from love (which, after all, is the essence of the 'supernatural splendor' of which we have been despoiled); everyone must first be healed and filled with God's gifts. But then everyone is also called to become a Samaritan—to follow Christ and become like him. (201)

Critique

Ratzinger's interpretation of the Samaritan as an image of Jesus is a huge backward step in the direction of outmoded scholarship, through which the parables were automatically allegorized. Luke's text in fact properly requires quite a different approach. The salient point of the story is to contrast two hard-hearted members of the Temple-clergy with the compassionate Samaritan. It tells of a person who has been attacked (v 30), with subsequent details: three different persons see his distress, and the first two pass him by without helping. The third, a despised foreigner, demonstrates self-sacrificing care (v 33). In this climactic verse, help moreover comes from the enemy—a source from whom neither the victim nor Jesus' hearers would have expected any compassion. The Samaritan is an enemy—an alien who puts Jews to shame. And although Ratzinger's introductory comment—"This was a perfectly realistic story" (196)—could have led to a reasonable interpretation based on historical fact, in the end he prefers to allegorize the parable. Once again he is inculcating doctrinal belief rather than exegetical method, which had been his initial promise.

Overview of pp. 202–11
The Parable of the Two Brothers . . .
(Luke 15:11–32)

Ratzinger begins his exposition with the remark, "Perhaps the most beautiful of Jesus' parables, this story is also known as the parable of the prodigal son" (202). And he proceeds to his customary sketch of the narrative content, with deference to exegesis of the Church Fathers (203–6).

At the center of the parable is the father, whose archetype Ratzinger finds in Hos 11:1–9. He summarizes the essence of the passage as follows: "Because God is God, the Holy One, he acts as no man could act. God has a heart, and this heart turns, so to speak, against God himself: Here in Hosea, as in the Gospel, we encounter once again the word *compassion*, which is expressed by means of the image of the maternal womb. God's heart transforms wrath and turns punishment into forgiveness" (206–7).

The next step is for Ratzinger to address how Jesus figures or enters into the parable. Augustine had seen Jesus in the paternal embrace (15:20), but Ratzinger rejects this idea. He sees the parable, by contrast, as Jesus' justification of "his own goodness towards sinners. . . . Attention to the historical context of the parable thus yields by itself an 'implicit Christology'" (207).

Turning to the second section of the parable, in which the father responds kindly to the older son's anger, Ratzinger concludes that the missing reaction of this bitter son would be simply inappropriate to the main message. Rather, the scene suddenly shifts, and "Jesus [uses] these words of the father to speak to the heart of the murmuring Pharisees and scribes who have grown indignant at his goodness to sinners (cf. Lk 15:2). It now becomes fully clear that Jesus identifies his goodness to sinners with the goodness in the parable and that all the words attributed to the father are the words that he himself addresses to the righteous" (209).

But that is not all, for according to Ratzinger the parable thus moves even beyond the historical moment in the life of Jesus when Jesus defended his actions against the objections of Pharisees and scribes: indeed, even here and now he "is wooing the hearts of his adversaries" (209). "In this parable, then, the Father through Christ is addressing us, the ones who never left home, encouraging us too to convert truly and to find joy in our faith" (211).

Critique

On pp. 206–7: The archetype of the father-figure cannot be found in Hos 11:1–9, for it is a text that speaks of God's relationship with and behavior toward the whole people of Israel, whereas Luke's parable describes a single father's way of dealing compassionately with two sons with varying behaviors, both lovingly accepted. This latter father is quite unlike Hosea's stern God.

On pp. 207–9: Ratzinger derives the historical context of this parable from its literary context, where it serves to illustrate Luke 15:1–2. Indeed, he seems to conflate the historical with the literary contexts, a highly questionable move, since Luke was no eyewitness. Moreover, the idea of God's goodness that is adumbrated in the parable has no perceptible connection with Jesus' table fellowship with sinners.

Overview of pp. 211–17
The Parable of the Rich Man and Lazarus
(Luke 16:19–31)

Ratzinger assures us that Psalms 44, 73, and 77—on the suffering poor confronted by rich cynics—contribute to a better understanding of the Lazarus-parable, in which "[t]he Lord wants to lead us from foolish cleverness toward true wisdom; he wants teach us to discern the real good. And so we have good grounds, even though it is not there in the text, to say that, from the perspective of the Psalms, the rich glutton [in the parable] was already an empty-hearted man in this world, and that his carousing was only an attempt to smother this interior emptiness of his. The next life only brings to life the truth already present in this life" (215).

Abraham is unable to send Lazarus to the rich man's house. "But at this point something strikes us. We are reminded of the resurrection of Lazarus of Bethany, recounted to us in John's Gospel. . . . The miracle leads not to faith, but to hardening of hearts" (216), as we read in John 11:45–53.

Ratzinger's then develops the Lazarus-scenario even further, first in the form of a question and incitement to make the proper comparison: "Do we not recognize in the figure of Lazarus—lying at the rich man's door covered in sores—the mystery of Jesus, who 'suffered outside the city walls' (Heb 13:12) and, stretched naked on the Cross, was delivered over to the mockery and contempt of the mob, his body 'full of blood and wounds'?" (216–17). He concludes with the overriding confession: "He, the true Lazarus, *has* risen from the dead—and he has come to tell us so" (217). It is the prelude, in fact, to the ultimate doxology of this section: "He, crucified and risen, is the true Lazarus. The parable is inviting us to believe and to follow him, God's great sign. But it is more than a parable. It speaks of reality, of the most decisive realty in all history" (217).

Critique

On pp. 216–17: This parable neither states, nor even implies, that Jesus' life is in any way suggested by the beggar Lazarus.

THE BOTTOM LINE: Ratzinger's one-sided christological interpretation of the parables of Jesus misses their content. The complexity of the parables is not so easily resolved and deserves more responsible treatment than the one we find in this book.

Chapter Ten
on Chapter 8
The Principal Images of John's Gospel

> Unwilling to acknowledge the widely
> recognized artificiality of John's gospel,
> Ratzinger is forced to claim historical
> validity for a clearly mythical portrait.

This chapter consists of two parts, "Introduction: The Johannine Question" and "The Principal Johannine Images." The latter is subdivided into the sections "Water," "Vine and Wine," "Bread," and "Shepherd."

Overview of pp. 218–38
Introduction: The Johannine Question

So far Ratzinger has devoted his attention mainly to the first three gospels. Now he turns "to the image of Jesus presented by the Fourth Evangelist, an image that in many respects seems quite different from that of the other Gospels" (218). In the Synoptics, Ratzinger observes, "the mystery of Jesus' oneness with the Father is ever present and determines everything, even though it remains hidden beneath his humanity" (218); in John, on the other hand, "Jesus' divinity appears unveiled" (219). These differences have led most Johannine scholars "to deny the historicity of the text—with the exception of the Passion narrative and a few details—and to regard it as a later theological reconstruction. It was said to express a highly developed Christology, but not to constitute a reliable source for knowledge of the historical Jesus" (219). One had to give up radical late datings and had to acknowledge that John was written in the late first century; yet questioning "of the Gospel's historical character . . . continued unabated" (219).

Ratzinger rejects Rudolf Bultmann's thesis that Gnosticism influenced John.[1] He approvingly quotes Martin Hengel: "In reality, there is no Gnostic redeemer myth in the sources which can be demonstrated chronologically to be pre-Christian" (220).[2] And he points to the fact that "Johannine scholarship in the generation after Bultmann took a radically different direction" (220), and accepted the assumption that the "Fourth Gospel rests on extraordinarily precise knowledge of times and places, and so can only have been produced by someone who had an excellent firsthand knowledge of Palestine at the time of Jesus" (220–21). Furthermore, it has become evident that "the Gospel thinks and argues entirely in terms of the Old Testament—of the Torah", being "deeply rooted in the Judaism of Jesus' times" (221).

Again following Martin Hengel, Ratzinger notes that its unliterary Greek was characteristic of the upper classes of Jerusalem of that time and points to the priestly aristocracy of Jerusalem as the source of the Gospel of John.[3] As a possible confirmation for this thesis he proposes the report in John 18:15–16: [15]"Now Simon Peter followed Jesus, and another disciple. And that disciple was known to the high priest, and he went with Jesus into the courtyard of the high priest. [16]But Peter stood outside at the door. the other disciple, who was known to the high priest, went out and spoke to the woman who kept the door, and brought Peter in."

Ratzinger now turns to two decisive issues in the Johannine question: "Who is the author of this Gospel? How reliable is it historically?" (222). With respect to the first issue it must be said that the beloved disciple—who according to the Gospel is its author (cf. John 19:34–35; 21:24)—is never identified by name. Against the view that this disciple is not an historical person but rather a symbol for a basic structure of faith (223), Ratzinger takes a firm stand: "If the favorite disciple in the Gospel expressly assumes the function of a witness to the truth of the events he recounts, he is presenting himself as a living person. He intends to vouch for historical events as a witness and he thus claims for himself the status of a historical figure. Otherwise the statements we have examined, which are decisive for the intention and the quality of the entire Gospel, would be emptied of meaning" (223).

Ratzinger then reminds the reader that church tradition since the early third century unanimously considered John the son of Zebedee to be the author of the Fourth Gospel. After that he summarizes modern objections to such a view by asking, "Can the fisherman from the Lake of Genesareth have written this sublime Gospel full of visions that peer into the deepest depth of God's mystery? Can he, the Galilean fisherman, have been as closely connected with the priestly aristocracy, its language, and its mentality as the Evangelist obviously is? Can he have been related to the family of the high priest, as the text hints (cf. Jn 18:15)? (224).

Drawing on a study by the French exegete Henri Gazelles, Ratzinger's finds it quite possible that "John Zebedee" was the son of a priest who twice a year performed his service at the temple in Jerusalem. Indeed, he agrees with Cazelles that the last supper of Jesus may have taken place "in the 'pied-à-terre' of the priest Zebedee, who 'lent the upper room to Jesus and the Twelve'" (225).

These deliberations lead Ratzinger to the conclusion that "in light of current scholarship, then, it is quite possible to see Zebedee's son John as the bystander who solemnly asserts his claim to be an eyewitness (cf. Jn 19:35) and thereby identifies himself as the true author of the Gospel" (225).

Still, "the complexity of the Gospel's redaction raises further questions" (225). In this respect it is important to consider a report of the bishop Papias of Hierapolis—who died around 220 CE—transmitted by church historian Eusebius (d. ca. 338 CE), that distinguishes between the apostle John and a presbyter with the same name. The latter was the leader of a "school of John" at Ephesus and the author of 2 John and 3 John.

> He must have been closely connected with the Apostle; perhaps he had even been acquainted with Jesus himself. After the death of the Apostle, he was identified wholly as the bearer of the latter's heritage, and in the collective memory, the two figures were effectively fused. At any rate, there seems to be grounds for ascribing to "Presbyter John" an essential role in the definitive shaping of the gospel, though he must have always regarded himself as the trustee of the tradition he had received from the son of Zebedee. (226)

Having thus solved the question of authorship, Ratzinger claims to have "taken a decisive step toward answering the question of the historical credibility of the Fourth Gospel" (227), and therefore assures us that this "Gospel ultimately goes back to an eyewitness, and even the actual redaction of the text was substantially the work of one of his closest followers within the living circle of his disciples" (227).

Ratzinger, however, criticizes the view that the Johannine School was the basis of further thinking about what had set the tone of Jesus' discourses with the Twelve. For "according to the text of the Gospel itself, what we find are not so much internal didactic discourses but rather Jesus' dispute with the Temple aristocracy" (227).

To Hengel's view that clearly "the evangelist is not narrating historical, banal recollections of the past but the rigorously interpretative spirit-paraclete leading into truth, which has the last word throughout the work,"[4] Ratzinger objects: "What does this contrast mean? What makes historical recollection banal? Is the truth of what is recollected important or not? And what sort of truth can the Paraclete guide into if he leaves behind the historical because it is too banal?" (228).

Ratzinger similarly objects to Ingo Broer's thesis that the Gospel of John is not an historical account but a witness to faith,[5] and gives it short shrift: "What faith does it 'testify' to if, so to speak, it has left history behind? How does it strengthen faith if it presents itself as a historical testimony—and does so quite emphatically—but then does not report history? I think we are dealing here with a false concept of the historical, as well as with a false concept of faith and of the Paraclete. A faith that discards history in this manner really turns to into 'Gnosticism.' It leaves flesh, incarnation—just what true history is—behind" (228).

Now Ratzinger becomes even more specific about the concept of "history" and "historical" and gives the following details:

> If "historical" is understood to mean that the discourses of Jesus transmitted to us have to be something like a recorded transcript in order to be acknowledged as "historically" authentic, then the discourses of John's Gospel are not "historical." But the fact that they make no claim to literal accuracy of this sort by no means implies that that they are merely "Jesus poems" that the members that the members of the Johannine school gradually put together, claiming to be acting under the guidance of the Paraclete. What the Gospel is really claiming is that it has correctly rendered the substance of the discourses, of Jesus' self-attestation in the great Jerusalem disputes, so that the readers really do encounter the decisive content of this message and, therein, the authentic figure of Jesus. (229)

Indeed, says Ratzinger, we are dealing with a "particular sort of historicity" (229) in the Fourth Gospel. To further elucidate this strange phrase Ratzinger again refers to Martin Hengel, who argued that along with John's theological concern, his personal recollection, and church tradition, historical data had shaped the text of the Gospel of John; but that its author violated historical reality because the Paraclete has the last word.[6] With this reconstruction, Ratzinger, strongly disagrees. "For how is the Paraclete supposed to have the last word if the Evangelist has already violated the actual history?" (229–30). Therefore, one should put the case thus: The Evangelist wanted to make an eyewitness report of what happened, and he drew partly from his own memory and partly from the first three gospels, with which he was no doubt familiar "in one or another version" (230). Besides, Church tradition and the guidance of the Holy Spirit added to this. Yet, "[h]owever much the author stands out as an individual witness, the remembering subject that speaks here is always the 'we' of the community of disciples, the 'we' of the Church. Because the personal recollection that provides the foundation of the Gospel is purified and deepened by being inserted into the memory of the Church, it does indeed transcend the banal recollection of facts" (231).

Ratzinger adduces John 2:17, John 2:22, and John 12:14–16 to explain the remembering of the disciples. This, he insists, "is a co-remembering in the 'we' of the Church . . . under the guidance of the Holy Spirit; by remembering, the believer enters into the depth of the event" and "comes to know it more deeply and thus sees the truth concealed in the outward act" (233). By way of illustration Ratzinger focuses on two passages from the infancy narratives in the Gospel of Luke.[7] In them, Mary "penetrates into the interior dimension, she sees the events in their inter-connectedness, and she learns to understand them" (234). Indeed, such a kind of "recollection" is typical of the Gospel of John; it is "no mere psychological or intellectual process; it is a pneumatic event . . . a being-led by the Holy Spirit, who shows us the connectedness of Scripture, the connection between word and reality" (234). This "also has some fundamental implications for the concept of inspiration" (234). Since the author of the Fourth Gospel "thinks and writes with the memory of the Church, the 'we' to which he belongs opens beyond the personal and is guided in its depths by the Spirit of God, who is the Spirit of truth" (234).

In summary, then, "the Gospel of John, because it is a 'pneumatic Gospel,' does not simply transmit a stenographic transcript of Jesus' words and ways; it escorts us . . . beyond the external into the depth of words and events that come from God and lead us back to him. As such the Gospel is 'remembering,' which means that it remains faithful to what really happened and is not a 'Jesus-poem,' not a violation of the historical events. . . . It shows us the real Jesus, and we can confidently make use of it as a source of information about him" (234–35).

Ratzinger adds two notes. For one thing, "John stands squarely on the foundation of the Old Testament" (235), for another, the Gospel "has a rhythm dictated by Israel's calendar of festivals" (236). "Only if we constantly keep in mind the liturgical context of Jesus' discourses, indeed of the whole structure of John's Gospel, will we be able to understand its vitality and depth. . . . It is evident that Jesus' discourses direct us toward worship and in this sense toward 'sacrament,' at the same time embracing the questioning and seeking of all peoples" (237–38).

Critique

On p. 219: Ratzinger is incorrect in arguing that modern exegetical research regards the Passion narrative of John as historically reliable. Most critical scholars have concluded that many elements of that narrative—for example, long passages in Pilate's interrogation (John 18:28–19:16) that go beyond the Markan account—are inventions. Besides, the report of Jesus' mother and the beloved disciple under the cross (John

19:26–27) is considered by most to be a fabrication. Only in the matter of placing Jesus' death on the day before Passover (the Synoptics put it on the first day of the Passover) do some argue that John may be correct.

On pp. 220–21: Ratzinger claims that the "extraordinarily precise knowledge of times and places" must be due to somebody who had first-hand knowledge of Palestine. Such a thesis is unwarranted, since the author may well have received these details from traditions available to him. Against Ratzinger's thesis one should adduce the grotesque stereotype of "the Jews" that occurs throughout the Gospel.[8] Further, John 11:49 and 18:13 are wrong in reporting a yearly succession in the office of the high priest.

On pp. 221–22: In the older tradition (Mark 14:54) we read that Peter followed Jesus to the court of the High Priest. The information given in John 18:15–16 explains that access was gained through a personal contact. But this is hardly evidence that Jesus' disciples included relatives of the priestly aristocracy.

On p. 223: Can Ratzinger fail to recognize that authors routinely create fictitious characters who represent themselves as living persons and as a trustworthy witnesses?

On p. 224: The objections raised in modern times against Irenaeus' identification of the apostle John with the author of the Fourth Gospel are more numerous and serious than Ratzinger lets on. For one thing, he fails to mention that the term "kingdom of God," which clearly constituted the center of Jesus' preaching, has little importance in John. For another, Mark 10:35–40, written about 70 CE, and thus a couple of decades before the Fourth Gospel, indicates that the apostle John had already suffered martyrdom. Besides, historical-critical scholars unanimously agree that John wrote his gospel on the basis of sources — whether the first three gospels or no longer extant sources; but this hardly comports with an eyewitness author. Further, Ratzinger's argument that a fisherman from Lake of Genesareth might have written such a sublime gospel and might have been familiar with the language and thought of the priestly aristocracy in Jerusalem is not convincing. Not only is it sheer speculation to imagine that John's father, Zebedee, performed priestly duties in Jerusalem, but even if such evidence existed, the idea that Zebedee offered Jesus and his disciples his own pied-à-terre for the last supper is likewise without a shred of support.

On pp. 225–27: Though Ratzinger correctly notes that the name "John" does not appear in 2 and 3 John, he gives the impression that "The Presbyter" who wrote these two letters was the presbyter John. The assertion that the latter played a decisive role in the shaping of the Gospel of John is an arbitrary modern idea that lacks any ancient testimony. The claim that that the presbyter John regarded himself as a trustee of what he had received from John the son of Zebedee is equally capricious.

On p. 227: Despite Ratzinger's attempt to paint them as "Jesus' dispute with the Temple authorities," John 13–16 are in fact four chapters of "internal didactic discourses."

On pp. 228–29: Ratzinger's dispute with Hengel and Broer reveals his way of dealing with the historical reports that John presents. Because *a priori* the Gospel of John cannot be tainted with Gnosticism, it must give a reliable account of Jesus. According to this "logic" everything is historical that claims to be historical—as long as it is part of the Bible.

On p. 229: Ratzinger tries to show that although the discourses of Jesus in the Fourth Gospel are not historical they are nonetheless "historical." Such a self-contradictory strategy is bound to fail. First, he writes that the discourses in the Gospel do not claim to reproduce the words of Jesus literally, but John 14:25–26 shows that to be false: [25]"I have spoken to you while I was with you. [26]But the Paraclete, the Holy Spirit, whom the Father will send in my name, he will teach you all things, and bring to your remembrance all that I have said to you." Second, the commonly accepted thesis that the Johannine discourses are Jesus-poems cannot be refuted by arguing that the author *intended* to report Jesus' discourses correctly. Everyone knows what is often paved with the best of intentions.

On pp. 231–35: Ratzinger's reflections on the topic "remember-remembrance" obscure the problem at hand. For the discourses of the Johannine Jesus are not only non-historical as compared to "stenographic transcripts" (235) but in both form and content they have nothing to do with the historical Jesus. The "memory of the Church" is unable to transform them retroactively into authentic words of Jesus. In a further offense to the human intellect, Ratzinger declares the memory of the Church to have as its source the Holy Spirit (236). According to this assertion, the dubious dogma of the divine inspiration of Scripture becomes in effect the validation of historical truth.

Overview of pp. 238–48
Water

In the section entitled "Water"—the beginning of the second division of chapter 8—Ratzinger first points out that water in general appears "in various forms and hence with various meanings" (238). After that he turns to a number of Johannine passages that deal with the topic "water."

Ratzinger interprets John 3:5 ("Unless one is born of water and Spirit, he cannot enter the kingdom of God") as follows:

> In order to be able to enter the Kingdom of God, man must be made new, he must become another person. . . . What does this mean? . . . Baptism, the gateway into communion with Christ, is being interpreted for us here as rebirth. This rebirth—by analogy with natural birth from the begetting of the man and the conception of the woman—involves a double principle: God's spirit and "water, the 'universal mother' of natural life—which grace raises up in the sacrament to be a sister-image of the virginal Theotokos."[9] . . . In the sacrament, water stands for the maternal earth, the holy Church, which welcomes creation into herself and stands in place of it. (239–40)

On John 4, the story about the encounter between Jesus and the woman from Samaria at Jacob's well, Ratzinger writes, "The Lord promises the Samaritan woman water that becomes in the one who drinks it a source springing up into eternal life (cf. Jn 4:14), so that whoever drinks it will never be thirsty again" (240). Besides, "the symbolism of the well is associated with Israel's history" (240). And to be sure, the biblical patriarch Jacob had provided water, "But there is a greater thirst in man . . . because it seeks a life that reaches out beyond the biological sphere" (241). Thus the "promise of new water and the promise of new bread . . . both reflect the other dimension of life, for which man can only yearn. John distinguishes between . . . biological life (*bios*) and the fullness of life (*zoé*) that is itself a source and so is not subject to the dying and becoming that mark the whole of creation" (241).

With regard to the miracle story in John 5:1–18 Ratzinger remarks that Jesus "accomplishes for the sick man the very thing the man had hoped to receive from the healing water" (241–42) hinting that chapter 7, "according to a convincing hypothesis of modern exegesis, in all likelihood originally followed directly after chapter 5" (242).

On the story in John 9 of the man born blind, Ratzinger underscores both Jesus' instruction that the man must wash in the Pool of Siloam and John's explanation that "Siloam means, being translated: the One Sent" (John 9:7). For Ratzinger, this is "more than a philological observation. It is a way of identifying the real cause of the miracle. For the 'One Sent' is Jesus. When all is said and done, Jesus is the one through whom and in whom the blind man is cleansed so that he can gain his sight. The whole chapter turns out to be an interpretation of Baptism, which enables us to see" (242).

Ratzinger's exposition of John 13:4–5, in which Jesus washes the feet of his disciples, is limited to the words: "The humility of Jesus, in making himself his followers' slave, is the purifying foot washing that renders us fit to take our places at God's table" (242).

According to John 19:34 a soldier pierced Jesus' side with a lance, whereupon blood and water came out. Concerning this report Ratzinger says, "There is no doubt that John means to refer here to the two main sacraments of the Church—Baptism and the Eucharist—which spring forth from Jesus' opened heart" (243). In contrast to this, he continues, the author has in 1 John 5:6–8 given the motif of blood and water a new twist:

> Here John very obviously gives the motif a polemical turn against a form of Christianity that acknowledges Jesus' Baptism as a saving event but does not acknowledge his death on the Cross in the same way.... So all that is left of Christianity is mere 'water'—without Jesus' bodiliness the word loses its power. Christianity becomes mere doctrine, mere moralism, an intellectual affair, but it lacks any flesh and blood. The redemptive character of Jesus' blood is no longer accepted. It disturbs the intellectual harmony. (243)

Next Ratzinger deals at some length with John 7:37–38, which he translates thus: [37]"On the last day of the feast, the great day, Jesus stood up and proclaimed, 'If anyone thirst, let him come to me and drink. [38]He who believes in me, as the Scripture has said, 'Out of his[10] heart shall flow rivers of living water'" (244). Ratzinger interprets this revelatory saying of Jesus against the background of the feast of Tabernacles. The water-rite executed during this festival had over the years become a remembrance of "the water from the rock that, in spite of all their doubts and fears, God gave the Jews as they wandered in the desert (cf. Num 20:1–13) . . . [and afterwards] increasingly became a motif of messianic hope.... On this pattern, the new Moses, the Messiah was expected to give these two essential gifts of life as well" (244). Therefore in John 7:37–38 Jesus declares himself to be the new Moses. Indeed, he "himself is the life-giving rock" (245).

Ratzinger now asks whether in John 7:38 the water is supposed to flow from the body of the believer or from that of Jesus and regards the latter as more plausible. Yet, he says, there need not be an opposition between the two options.

Be that as it may, an essential clue for the passage in question lies in the phrase "as the Scripture says" (John 7:38). Ratzinger takes a look at it and asks where in Scripture the term "living water" occurs. "Jesus attaches great importance to being in continuity with the Scripture, in continuity with God's history with men. The whole Gospel of John, . . . and the entirety of the New Testament writings, justify faith in Jesus by showing that all the currents of Scripture come together in him" (246). With respect to the question of where Scripture speaks of "living water (spring)" Ratzinger answers: "John is obviously not thinking of any one particular passage, but precisely of 'the Scripture,' of a vision that runs through its texts" (246). Traces of this vision appear not only in the account of the water-giving rock (Numbers 20, see above) but also in the vision of the new temple in Ezek 47:1–12 and further in Zech 13:1 and 14:8 (246–47). Rev 22:1 "reinterprets these images and at the same time manifests their greatness for the first time" (247).

Then follows a meditation in which the body of Jesus, the new temple, the living water and the New Jerusalem are brought into relation. Ratzinger sums up his thoughts thus:

> If one looks at history with a keen eye, one can see this river flowing through the ages from Golgotha, from Jesus crucified and risen. One can see that, wherever this river reaches, the earth is decontaminated and fruit-bearing trees grow up; one can see that life, real life, flows from this spring of love that has given itself and continues to give itself. (247–48)

Critique

On pp. 239–48: This section swarms with inaccuracies. In the exegesis of John 3:5, for example, Ratzinger's claim that the water in the sacrament is raised to the sister-image of the virginal Theotokos (240) is at best misleading. Equally far-fetched, and indeed totally unsupported by the text is his statement that the story of the healing of a man blind from birth in John 9 "turns out to be an interpretation of Baptism, which enables us to see" (242). Above all, one must object that Ratzinger's reflections on water symbolism in the Fourth Gospel derive from Johannine theology (along with its Old Testament presuppositions and later history) and not from the historical Jesus. Even if the two cannot be separated as neatly as modern scholarship proposes, it is passing strange that a book purporting "to portray the Jesus of the Gospels as the real, 'historical' Jesus in the strict sense of the word" (xxii) should focus so heavily on three such arcane issues as a) an aside of the Evangelist (John 9:7); b) his report on what happened to the body of Jesus (John 19:34); and c) post-Easter controversies about the salvific meaning of Jesus' death (1 John 5:6–8).

Overview of pp. 248–63

Vine and Wine

After some initial explanations about bread, wine, and oil as "gifts typical of Mediterranean culture" (248), Ratzinger turns to the story of Jesus' transformation of water into wine (John 2:1–12). He suggests that the chronological reference in v 1 ("on the third day") has a symbolic meaning and explains that Jesus' "hour which has not yet come" (v 4) points to the hour of the cross and of the glorification. "When at this juncture Jesus speaks to Mary of his hour, he is connecting the present moment with the mystery of the Cross interpreted as his glorification. . . . And yet Jesus has the power to anticipate this 'hour' in a mysterious sign. This stamps the miracle of Cana as an anticipation of the hour, tying the two intrinsically" (251). Ratzinger adds, "this thrilling mystery of the anticipated hour continues to occur again and again" (251). In the eucharist "in response to the Church's prayer, the Lord anticipates his return; he comes already now; he celebrates the marriage feast with us here and now. In so doing, he lifts us out of our time toward the coming 'hour'" (252).

In that respect Ratzinger sees a parallel in Mark 2:19 where Jesus explains why his disciples do not fast by saying: "Can the wedding guests fast so long as the bridegroom is among them?" Thus "he mysteriously places his own existence, himself, within the mystery of God. In him, in an unexpected way, God and man become one, become a 'marriage,' though this marriage . . . passes through the Cross, through the 'taking away' of the bridegroom" (252).

Now Ratzinger returns to the miracle story in John 2. Transforming water, which serves ritual needs, into wine "brings to light something of the fulfillment of the Law that is accomplished in Jesus' being and doing" (253). Ultimately, ritual purification is "never sufficient to make man capable of God"; but when water becomes wine, "[m]an's own efforts now encounter the gift of God, who gives himself and thereby creates the feast of joy that can only be instituted by the presence of God and his gift" (253).

In the next paragraph Ratzinger tells his readers that the history of religions research has found parallels between John 2 and the pagan myth of Dionysos. Besides, he informs us, Philo of Alexandria demythologized the story by replacing Dionysos with the Logos, who is then merged with the priest Melchisedek in Genesis 14. While it is doubtful that John had these connections in mind, Ratzinger concedes, one still may argue thus:

> But since Jesus himself in interpreting his mission referred to in Psalm 110, which features the priesthood of Melchisedek (cf. Mk 12:35–37); since the Letter to the Hebrews, which is theologically akin to the Gospel of John, explicitly develops a theology of Melchisedek; since John presents Jesus as the Logos of God and as God himself; since, finally, the Lord gave bread and wine as the bearers of the New Covenant, it is certainly not forbidden to think in terms of such connections and so to see shining through the Cana story the mystery of

the Logos and of his cosmic liturgy, which fundamentally transforms the myth of Dionysus, and yet also brings it to its hidden truth.[11] (254)

Now Ratzinger turns to the discourse in John 15 in which Jesus claims to be the vine. To properly understand this discourse, he avers, we ought to examine a "foundational Old Testament text based on the vine motif and to ponder briefly a related parable in the Synoptics" (254).

The example from the Old Testament is Isa 5:1–7, a "song" about a vineyard. Ratzinger attributes it to a specific historical situation: "The Prophet probably sang it in the context of the Feast of Tabernacles" [254]); then he paraphrases the text and then allegorizes it as a threat "of God's abandonment of Israel" (255).

The Synoptic parallel is Mark 12:1–12, in which Jesus "on the eve of his Passion" (256) has taken up Isaiah's song about a vineyard. Ratzinger complains that modern exegesis connects this parable only with the rejection of Jesus' message by his contemporaries and with his death on the cross. On the contrary, he protests, "the Lord always speaks in the present and with an eye to the future. He is also speaking with us and about us. If we open our eyes, isn't what is said in the parable actually a description of our present world? Isn't this precisely the logic of the modern age, of our age? Let us declare that God is dead, then we ourselves will be God. . . . The 'vineyard' belongs to us. What happens to man and the world next? We are already beginning to see it. . . ." (257).

In contrast to Isaiah's pessimistic forecast, Ratzinger finds an element of promise in Mark 12:9: the vineyard will be given to other servants. But "[t]his threat-promise applies not only to the ruling classes, about whom and with whom Jesus is speaking. It continues to apply among the new People of God as well—not, of course, to the whole Church, but repeatedly to the particular churches" (258). However, the threat-promise is followed "by a promise of a much more fundamental nature. The Lord cites Ps 118:22f: 'The stone which the builders rejected has become the cornerstone'" and thereby predicts "his Cross and Resurrection . . . [t]he indirect Christology of the early parables is transcended here into a fully open Christological statement" (258)

After these comments on Isa 5:1–12 and Mark 12:1–12, Ratzinger finally approaches the text of John 15 and at the opening focuses on its first sentence: "I am the true vine." On this Ratzinger comments: "The Son identifies himself with the vine; he himself has become the vine. He has let himself be planted in the earth. He has entered into the vine: The mystery of the Incarnation, which John spoke of in the prologue to his Gospel, is taken up again here in a surprising new way. . . . In the

Son, he himself [=God] has become the vine; he has forever identified himself, his very being, with the vine" (259). Indeed, the vine as a christological title "embodies a whole ecclesiology. The vine signifies Jesus' inseparable oneness with his own, who through him and with him are all 'vine,' and whose calling is to 'remain' in the vine" (260). "The vine . . . can no longer be uprooted or handed over to be plundered. It does, however, constantly need purification. . . . When man and his institutions climb too high, they need to be cut back; what has become too big must be brought back to the simplicity and poverty of the Lord himself" (260–61).

Further, Ratzinger says, one has to remember that Jesus tells this parable in the context of the Last Supper. "It is hard to believe that in his discourse on the vine he is not tacitly alluding to the new vine . . . which he now gives to us—the wine that would flow from his Passion. . . . In this sense the parable of the vine has a thoroughly eucharistic background" (261).

Finally Ratzinger emphasizes that the fruit Jesus expects from us is love. Pointing out that in John 15:1–10 the word "remain" is used ten times, he adds that part of this love "is this 'remaining,' which is profoundly connected with the kind of faith that holds on to the Lord and does not let go" (262). And an important element of this remaining is prayer (262).

Critique

On pp. 250–54: In the exegesis of the wine miracle in John 2, Ratzinger does not deal with the problems raised by the assumption that this account reflects an historical event. And the supposedly symbolic meaning of the time reference "on the third day" (250–51) is irrelevant to the historical Jesus, for it presupposes his divine prescience. In his exposition of this non-authentic reference to the hour that has not yet come (v 4), Ratzinger enumerates important aspects of the intent of John (251), but leads the reader astray by finding in it a reference to the Eucharist (251–52). To be sure, one cannot contradict his proposal that "it is certainly not forbidden to think" of the story of the wine miracle as having brought the myth of Dionysos "to its hidden truth" (254). But besides being a risibly empty double negative, it contributes nothing to our understanding of the historical Jesus.

On pp. 256–58: Ratzinger mistakenly regards Mark's parable of the Wicked Tenants (with its allegorical reference to the death of Jesus, see above, pp. 72–74) as authentic, applies to it an invalid exegetical method, and derives inadmissible results. For one thing, the parable has nothing to do with the problem of modern atheism. For another, the differentiation between the whole Church and particular churches is also utterly unrelated to the content of the parable. Furthermore, Ratzinger imagines it possible to distinguish between early and late parables of the historical Jesus, and thus feels free to assume that the New Testament gospels present a correct chronology of the life of Jesus. But critical scholarship laid that view to rest more than a century ago. It is now understood that the authors of the gospels arranged the pieces of traditions available to them in the order that they considered theologically appropriate. A yet more specific objection that strikes at the heart of his fuzzy allegorizing is the fact that the Gospel of Thomas (Saying 65)[12] presents a version of the Wicked Tenants that by omitting the allusion to Isaiah's "song of the vineyard" effectively removes the allegorical overtones and the christological elements as well. Has Ratzinger's investigation of modern scholarship carefully excluded Thomas? Or does he think that non-canonical gospels, even though probably very early, are irrelevant? In either case he does his readers a disservice and casts doubt on his credibility.

Overview of pp. 263-72
Bread

At the outset Ratzinger reminds the reader that he had already turned his attention to the bread-motif in connection with Jesus' temptations and the fourth petition of the Our Father (263). After that he recapitulates the feeding miracles in the Synoptics[13] and then turns to the Johannine version of that story (John 6:1–15) in order "to focus upon the interpretation that Jesus gives of this event in his great bread of life discourse" (264). He does not want to go into the details, he says, but only "to draw out its principal message and, above all, to situate it in the context of the whole tradition to which it belongs and in terms of which it has to be understood" (264).

Important for an understanding of the bread discourse is "the contrast between Moses and Jesus. Jesus is the definitive, greater Moses—the 'prophet' whom Moses foretold in his discourse at the border of the Holy Land" (264), and to whom the word of God in Deut 18:18[14] refers. Therefore, we are told, it is no accident that in John 6:14 and 7:40 Jesus is emphatically called "the prophet."

Completing the picture of Moses "is the only way to focus upon John's picture of Jesus" (265). Moses had spoken with God (Exod 33:11) but he was not allowed to see God's face (Exod 33:18, 22–23). In contrast to this, John 1:18 shows that Jesus "truly speaks from his vision of the Father, from unceasing dialogue with the Father, a dialogue that is his life" (265–66). Ratzinger continues: "Connected with this are two further gifts to Moses that attain their final form in Christ": first, the revelation of the name of God (cf. John 17:6) and second, the gift of Torah. "Israel realized with increasing clarity that this was Moses' fundamental and enduring gift, that what really set Israel apart was this knowledge of God's will and so of the right path of life" (266). Yet, because we have a "one-sided view of the Law, arising from a one-sided interpretation of Pauline theology," we fail to see "this joy of Israel: the joy of knowing God's will, and so of being privileged to live in accordance with God's will" (266). We must further observe that "as Jewish thought developed inwardly, it became increasingly plain that the real bread from heaven that fed and feeds Israel is precisely the Law—the word of God" (267).

It is against such a background that the bread discourse of John 6 should be read. Though it is true that Torah is bread from God, "it shows us only God's back, so to speak. It is 'a shadow'" (267). Yet from John 6:33 and 6:35 one sees who the true bread of God and of life is—Jesus. In him Torah has become a *person*. "When we encounter Jesus, we feed on the living God himself, so to speak; we truly eat 'bread from heaven'" (268). This bread "cannot be 'earned' by human work, by one's own achievement. It can only come to us as a gift from God, as *God's work* . . . in the context of faith in Jesus, who is dialogue—a living relationship with the father—and who wants to become Word and love in us as well" (268).

However, the question of how to "feed" on God has not been fully answered. "God becomes 'bread' for us first of all in the Incarnation of the Logos. . . . Yet a further step is still needed beyond even the Incarnation of the Word. Jesus names this step in the concluding words of his discourse: His flesh is life 'for' the world (Jn 6:51). Beyond the act of the Incarnation, this points to its intrinsic goal and ultimate realization: Jesus' act of giving himself up to death and the mystery of the Cross" (268–69). Even more specific is John 6:53, "where the Lord adds he will give us his blood to 'drink'." This phrase points "to what underlies the Eucharist: the sacrifice of Jesus, who sheds his blood for us, and in so doing steps out of himself, so to speak, pours himself out, and gives himself to us" (269).

From this it follows that there is no antagonism between "the Easter theology of the Synoptics and Saint Paul, on the one hand, and Saint John's supposedly purely incarnational theology, on the other" (269). For the incarnation "spoken of by the prologue is precisely the offering of his body on the Cross, which the sacrament makes accessible to us" (269). Thus in John 6 the Eucharist is put in the center of Christian existence. "At the same time, however, the Eucharist is revealed as man's unceasing great encounter with God, in which the Lord gives himself as 'flesh,' so that . . . we may become 'spirit.' Just as he was transformed through the Cross into a new manner of bodiliness and of being-human pervaded by God's own being, so too for us this food must become an opening out of our existence, a passing through the Cross, and an anticipation of the new life in God and with God" (270).

For that reason Jesus says at the end of the discourse, "It is the spirit that gives life, the flesh is of no avail" (John 6:63). "This in no way diminishes the realism of 'becoming flesh.' Yet the Paschal perspective of the sacrament is underlined. Only through the Cross and through the transformation that it effects does this flesh become accessible to us, drawing us up into the process of transformation" (270).

Before leaving the topic of bread, Ratzinger turns his attention to John 12:24: "Unless a grain of wheat falls into the earth and dies, it remains alone; but if it dies, it bears much fruit." Ratzinger reminds us that Jesus speaks this word "on Palm Sunday as he looks ahead to the universal Church" (271). Indeed, what "we call 'bread' contains the mystery of the Passion" (271). For the existence of bread presupposes that the grain of wheat must "be placed in the earth, it has to 'die,' and then the new ear can grow out of this death" (271).

At the end of the section on this Johannine motif, Ratzinger reports on the conversion of English writer C. S. Lewis. One day Lewis overheard an atheist concede "that the evidence for the historicity of the Gospels was actually surprisingly good. . . . 'About the dying God. Rum thing. It almost looks as if it really happened once'[15]" (271). Ratzinger adds in a triumphant tone:

> Yes, it really did happen. Jesus is no myth. He is a man of flesh and blood and he stands as a fully real part of history. We can go to the very places where he himself went. We can hear his words through his witnesses. He died and he is risen. It is as if the mysterious Passion contained in bread had waited for him, had stretched out his arms toward him; it is as if the myths had waited for him, because in him what they long for came to pass. The same is true of the wine. It too contains the Passion in itself, for the grape had to be pressed in order to become wine." (271-72)

Critique

On pp. 264–71: The so-called bread discourse of Jesus in John 6:26–58 presupposes the story of the miraculous feeding of the Five Thousand in John 6:1–15, but that account has no historical value. Besides, the Johannine bread discourse was originally not connected with the story of a miraculous feeding; this is clear from the synoptic parallels,[16] which have no bread discourse. Therefore the bread discourse in the Fourth

Gospel is not historical and cannot be used to attest to Jesus' self-understanding. In addition, the eucharistic section John 6:51c–58, like John 21, is an appendix—and even Ratzinger subsequently recognizes John 21 to be an appendix (276).

On p. 272: The statement that the mysterious Passion contained in bread and the myths have waited for Jesus derives from a bizarre theological point of view and has nothing to do with the historical Jesus.

Overview of pp. 272–86
The Shepherd

Ratzinger begins this section with general remarks about the motif of the shepherd in the Near East (the king as shepherd) and in the Old Testament (God as Israel's Shepherd), and quotes from Psalm 23 ("the Lord is my shepherd") and from Ezekiel 34–37, according to which God will gather the scattered sheep (272–73). After that Ratzinger turns to the parable of the lost sheep (Matt 18:12–14/Luke 15:4–7) and comments: "Jesus puts this parable as a question to his adversaries: Have you not read God's word in Ezekiel? I am only doing what God, the true Shepherd, foretold: I wish to seek out the sheep that are lost and bring the strayed back home" (273–74).

Now Ratzinger points out that according to Matt 26:31 "after the Last Supper, Jesus tells his disciples that the prophecy foretold in Zechariah 13:7 is about to be fulfilled: 'I will strike the shepherd, and the sheep of the flock will be scattered'" (274). Indeed, he says, this vision of the slain shepherd who through his death becomes the Savior has a close connection with Zech 12:10–11: ". . . And they will look on him whom they have pierced. . . . On that day the mourning in Jerusalem will be as great as the mourning for Hadad-Rimmon in the plain of Megiddo." While it is true that Hadad-Rimmon was one of the dying and rising vegetation deities whom Israel despised and regarded as a nothing, "yet, through the ritual lamentations over him, he [=the prophet] mysteriously prefigures someone who really does exist" (275).

Moreover, at this point Ratzinger sees an inner connection "with the Servant of God in Deutero-Isaiah" and quotes Karl Elliger: Zechariah's "gaze penetrates with remarkable accuracy into a new distance and circles around the figure of the one who was pierced on the cross at Golgotha. Admittedly, he does not clearly discern the figure of Christ"[17] (275). While Matthew's Jesus picks up Zech 13:7 at the beginning of the passion narrative, John, "by contrast, concludes his account of the Lord's Crucifixion [John 13:37] with an allusion to Zechariah 12:10: 'They shall look on him whom they have pierced'"(275). He combines this "with

Zechariah's prophetic vision of the fountain that purifies from sin and impurity" (John 19:34; cf. Zech 13:1) and with "the image of the Paschal Lamb [John 19:36], whose blood has purifying power" (275–76). In this way, "the circle is closed, joining the end to the beginning of the Gospel, where the Baptist—catching sight of Jesus—said: 'Behold, the Lamb of God, who takes away the sin of the world'" (Jn 1:29). The image of the lamb . . . thus encompasses the entire Gospel. It also points to the deepest meaning of the shepherd discourse, whose center is precisely Jesus' act of laying down his life" (276).

Now Ratzinger turns to John 10, though here Jesus does not at first identify himself with the shepherd (John 10:11) but with the door (John 10:7). Therefore Ratzinger connects the two images and afterwards examines "the appendix to the Gospel in chapter 21" and—rather obliquely referring again to the word "door"—notes Peter's appointment to the office of shepherd (John 21:15–17) (276–77).

Ratzinger derives from John 10 "four essential points"(278):

1. Jesus' promise is life in abundance (cf. John 10:10: "I came that they may have life, and have it abundantly"). While all human beings want life in abundance it is Jesus who promises to lead them to the "springs of life." "Man lives on truth and on being loved; on being loved by the truth. He needs God, the God who draws close to him, interprets for him the meaning of life, and thus points him toward the path of life" (279).

2. The second point concerns the motif that the shepherd gives his own life. "The Cross is at the center of the shepherd discourse. And it is portrayed not as an act of violence that takes Jesus unawares and attacks him from the outside, but a free gift of his very self" (280).

3. The third point is devoted to the saying about the mutual knowing of shepherd and flock (John 10:3–4, 14–15). It consists of meditations about the terms "knowing" and "belonging." "The mutual knowing of shepherd and sheep is interwoven with the mutual knowing of Father and Son. . . . Jesus' 'own' are woven into the Trinitarian dialogue" (282).

4. The fourth point, which focuses on the topic of the gathering of the sheep into one flock (John 10:16), focuses on a quotation from Ezek 37:15–17, 21–22 (God gathers the divided Israel). Jesus picks up this vision and enlarges it to include the Gentiles (cf. Matt 28:19; Acts 1:8). Therefore, one must say, "The Logos who became man in Jesus is the Shepherd of all men" (284).

A few remarks on the history of interpretation of the shepherd discourse in the ancient church then round off the section on the shepherd motif, and thus also the chapter about the "Principal Images of John's Gospel."

Critique

On pp. 273–74: It is unlikely that Jesus intended to apply the image of the shepherd in the parable of the lost sheep to himself. On this see Matt 18:12–14 and especially the parallel in Luke 15:4–7, which does not mention a shepherd, and note the latter's parallel incident in Luke 15:8–10. Besides, the promises of Ezekiel do not form the background for this parable: The prophet refers to a scattered flock, whereas Jesus speaks about a single lost animal. Ratzinger is, to say the least, rather impressionistic in the matter of perceiving similarities. Nearly any resemblance can be made to serve his homiletic purposes.

On pp. 274–75: Jesus did not say the words attributed to him in Matt 26:31 (=Mark 14:27). Instead, early Christians created this speech and put it on his lips in order to persuade themselves and others that he foresaw both his death and the flight of the disciples (Mark 14:50). A further purpose was to emphasize the belief that Jesus' suffering was in accordance with the Scriptures. The notion that Hadad-Rimmon is a mysterious prefiguration of Jesus has no historical basis whatever.

On pp. 276–84: Jesus' discourse in John 10:1–18 presupposes his awareness of the details of his death and resurrection (10:17–18), as well the existence of a church consisting of both Jews and Gentiles. Therefore it cannot possibly go back to Jesus of Nazareth.

THE BOTTOM LINE: Ratzinger's comments on the author of the Fourth Gospel are speculative, theological, and in some ways arbitrary. In the final analysis he fails to present a single valid argument against the overwhelming consensus of New Testament scholars that the discourses of Jesus in this Gospel bear no resemblance to anything the historical Jesus said. As so often in his book, Ratzinger claims to present the portrait of a real person but delivers instead a fanciful divine figure for the purposes of bolstering centuries of institutional doctrine and canonized myth.

Chapter Eleven
on Chapter 9
Peter's Confession and the Transfiguration[1]

In subscribing to the historicity of the transfiguration story and the passion predictions, Ratzinger privileges church doctrine over the scholarly exegesis he promised.

Overview of pp. 287–305
Peter's Confession

In the first three gospels, Peter's confession (Mark 8:27–30; Matt 16:13–20; Luke 9:18–21) is followed by Jesus' foretelling of his passion and resurrection, and his definition of discipleship (Mark 8:31–34; Matt 16:21–24; Luke 9:22–23). "These three elements—Peter's words and Jesus' twofold answer—belong inseparably together" (288).

Ratzinger explains how Peter's confession is placed within the context of each gospel (288–91), adding: "All three Synoptics agree in recounting the opinion of the people that Jesus is John the Baptist, or Elijah, or some other of the prophets returned from the dead" (291). The catchword "opinion" is an occasion for Ratzinger to move to the present. "Today, too, similar opinions are clearly held by the 'people' who have somehow or other come to know Christ, who have perhaps even made a scholarly study of him, but have not encountered Jesus himself in his utter uniqueness and otherness" (292). For example the philosopher "Karl Jaspers spoke of Jesus alongside Socrates, the Buddha, and Confucius as one of the four paradigmatic individuals" (292). Thus nowadays "it is fashionable to regard Jesus as one of the great religious founders who were granted a profound experience of God" (293). Yet, it is only a finite, human experience of God. "It is man, the individual subject, who ends up being himself the measure.... There is no definitive commitment here" (293).

Now Ratzinger returns to the gospel texts and continues: "Standing in marked contrast to the opinion of the people is the 'recognition' of the disciples, which expresses itself in acknowledgment, in confession"

(293). In each gospel, though, this confession is differently formulated: Mark 8:29, "You are the Christ"; Luke 9:20, "You are the Christ of God"; Matthew 16:16, "You are the Christ, the Son of the living God"; John 6:69, "You are the Holy One of God."

In what follows Ratzinger repudiates the view that Peter's confession derives from the Easter situation rather than from the life of Jesus, and denies that it stemmed from an experience similar to that of Paul on the Damascus road when he was called to be an apostle (294–96). The statement of Acts 1:21–22 makes it clear that the first apostles were called during the lifetime of Jesus, "and this continuity explains why the commission given to Peter is actually fundamentally different from the commission given to Paul" (297). This means that Ratzinger reads Luke-Acts as normative.

After that Ratzinger explains the distinction between two types of confessional formula, the "substantive" and the "verbal." "All three forms of Peter's confession transmitted to us by the Synoptics are 'substantive'—you *are* the Christ, the Christ of God, the Christ, the Son of the living God" (298). At the same time, a "verbal" confession is set "alongside these substantive statements: the prophetic announcement of the Paschal Mystery of Cross and Resurrection" (298).

As for the title of Christ used in Peter's confession, "the respective form of the title must be read within the total context of the individual Gospels and the specific form in which they have been handed down" (299). In Mark 14:61 the question of the high priest picks up the title "Christ"; Simeon's words in Luke 2:26 re-echo in Peter's confession and the mockery hurled at the crucified Jesus (Luke 23:35) is a counter image of it; the confession of "Matthew's" Peter corresponds to that of the disciples (13:33). Therefore, one may say, "In various ways, the disciples were repeatedly able to sense in Jesus the presence of the living God himself" (302).

After looking at the Johannine version of Peter's confession (John 6:68–69) Ratzinger formulates the result of his investigation as follows: "[T]he attempt to arrive at a historical reconstruction of Peter's original words and then to attribute everything else to posterior developments, and possibly to post-Easter faith, is very much on the wrong track" (303), and he poses a question by way of proof: "Where is post-Easter faith supposed to have come from if Jesus laid no foundation for it before Easter?" (303).[2] He ends with what he sees as a sound conclusion: "Scholarship overplays its hand with such reconstructions" (303).

Political messianism was not the issue during the trial of Jesus before the Sanhedrin, Ratzinger argues, but rather his "putting himself on an equal footing with the living God himself. This was what the strictly monotheistic faith of the Jews was unable to accept. This was the idea to which even Jesus could only slowly and gradually lead people. This was also what permeated his entire message—while preserving unbroken unity with faith in the one God; this was what was new, characteristic, and unique about his message" (303–4).

What the disciples came to recognize during Jesus' lifetime is that "he is more than, and different from 'one of the Prophets.' . . . He is *the* Prophet who like Moses, speaks face-to-face with God as with a friend; he is the Messiah, but in a different sense from that of a mere bearer of some commission from God" (304).

Ratzinger describes their experience thus: "At certain key moments, the disciples came to the astonishing realization: This is God himself. They were unable to put all this together into a perfect response. Instead they rightly drew upon the Old Testament's words of promise: Christ, the Anointed One, Son of God, Lord. These are the key words on which their confession focused, while still tentatively searching for a way forward. It could arrive at its complete form only when Thomas, touching the wounds of the Risen Lord, cried out, in amazement: 'My Lord and my God'" (304–5).

Then follows an application of this to the church of today: "In the end, however, these words send us upon a never-ending journey. They are so vast that we can never grasp them completely, and they always surpass us. Throughout her entire history, the pilgrim Church has been exploring them ever more deeply. Only by touching Jesus' wounds and encountering his Resurrection are we able to grasp them, and then they become our mission" (305).

Critique

On p. 297: Acts cannot be used as evidence for the thesis that Jesus called twelve apostles who recognized Jesus as divine. For one thing, Luke, the author, writes from a later, third generation perspective; for another, we learn from the primary source contained in 1 Cor 15:5 that Christ appeared to Cephas (Peter) and the Twelve. This "appearance" constitutes the first phase of Easter faith, while a second phase is reflected in Christ's "appearance" to James and all the apostles (1 Cor 15:7). Luke afterwards combines "the Twelve" and "the Apostles" together with the result that we now have twelve apostles. Finally, none of these texts mentions or even implies the equality of Jesus and God.

On pp. 303–4: Jesus did not put himself on equal footing with the living God in the hearing before the Sanhedrin. a) There were no witnesses to this supposed event, and the statements in question (Mark 14:61–62)[3] are a compendium of Mark's view of Jesus as the Christ, the Son of God *and* the Son of man. Ever since Mark 1:1, the author's matter-of-course assumption has been that Jesus is the Christ. In 9:4 those who follow Jesus are described as those belonging to Christ. In 8:29 Peter confesses Jesus as Christ. Jesus is called the son of the most Blessed, that is, of God, not only at the beginning of the Gospel (1:1) but also at his baptism (1:11), at the transfiguration (9:7), and is so recognized by demons (3:11; 5:7).

b) The hearing before the Sanhedrin was composed on the basis of a narrative tradition about the hearing before Pilate (Mark 15:1–20), and therefore cannot be regarded as an historical account. In any case, the Sanhedrin was barred by law from convening at night.

On pp. 304–5: The story of the doubting Thomas (John 20:24–29) does not belong to the first Christian generation. As a later fabrication, it cannot be used to describe the faith of its earliest members. An exegetical demonstration follows:

John 20:24–29

The appearance of the "Risen One" to Thomas

[24]One of the twelve, Thomas, called the Twin, was not with them when Jesus came, [25a]and so the other disciples told him, "We have seen the Lord." [25b]He said, "Unless I see the marks where the nails were in his hands, and put my finger where the nails were, and my hand in his side, I will not believe." [26a]Eight days later, the disciples were in the house once again, and Thomas was with them. [26b]Even though the doors were shut, Jesus entered and stood in their midst, saying, "Peace be with you." [27]Then he says to Thomas, "Put out your finger, here are my hands; and reach out with your hand, and place it in my side; be doubtful no longer, but believe." [28]Thomas replied to him, "My Lord and my God!" [29a]Jesus said, "Is it because you have seen me that you now believe? [29b]Blessed are those who have never seen me and (yet) believe."

Not only does this story have no parallel in the Synoptics, but it conflicts with the preceding section, vv 19–23, which gave no indication that any of the disciples were absent when Jesus appeared.

Verse 24: This verse, with its explicit reference to verse 19, explains why Jesus had not yet appeared to Thomas. Thomas and his nickname "Twin" (in Greek, *didymos*) were previously mentioned in 11:16, and there he also played the role of skeptic.

Verse 25a: 'We have seen the Lord' echoes "when they saw the Lord" (20:20b) and thus naturally comports with Mary Magdalene's speech in 20:18.

Verse 25b: The conditions stipulated by Thomas hark back to 20:20a.

Verse 26a: The note of time, "eight days later", places this new gathering, like the first one (verse 19), on a Sunday.

Verse 26b: This verse is a nearly verbatim rehearsal of 20:19b; the closed doors are taken from 20:19a.

Verse 27: Jesus' invitation reiterates Thomas' wish in verse 25b. John considers the earthly Jesus to have been omniscient[4], and the "Risen One" even more so. (For touching as evidence of Jesus' identity and the reality of his body, see Luke 24:39–43.)

Verse 28: Rather than accept Jesus' invitation, Thomas offers the appropriate confession to the "Risen One,"[5] recognizing God as present in Jesus. Furthermore, "My Lord and my God" amounts to a reformulation of the identification expressed in 1:1 and 1:18.[6]

Verse 29a: The form of Jesus' question recalls 1:50; in its note of reproach it resembles 3:10; 6:61; and 14:9a.

Verse 29b: This beatitude, restating a theme also found in 4:48, is the final speech that John attributes to the risen Jesus. Exploring the relationship between seeing and believing is typical of the evangelist.[7]

Ultimately then, since John has created this narrative to dramatize the same motif of doubt that we find in other resurrection stories,[8] its historical value is nil. We may justifiably follow the late Anton Dauer in concluding that the evangelist "has attached to the figure of Thomas the theme of the disciples' unbelief, its overthrow by an encounter with the Risen Lord, and an examination of the problematical value of such faith."[9] Apparently he relocated the motif of doubt from John 20:19–23 to this later narrative.

At the same time, though, the question remains why John felt he needed to use Thomas to spell out his own belief in the bodily resurrection of Jesus. It seems most likely that he was at pains to defend his belief against rival Christian groups of a gnostic persuasion, whose members separated the spiritual Christ—the only one who in their eyes mattered—from the human Jesus.[10]

Overview of pp. 305–18
The Transfiguration

At the outset Ratzinger asks whether the time reference attached to the transfiguration of Jesus (Matt 17:1/Mark 9:2: "after six days"; Luke 9:28: "after about eight days") alludes to the weeklong feast of Tabernacles, which follows six days after the feast of Atonement, or whether the transfiguration story should be read against the background of Exodus 24—Moses' ascent to mount Sinai (305–8).

Ratzinger notes that just as earlier in the Sermon on the Mount and in the nights spent by Jesus in prayer, the mountain represents God's nearness.

> Once again we need to keep together in our minds the various mountains of Jesus' life: the mountain of the temptation; the mountain of his great preaching; the mountain of his prayer; the mountain of the Transfiguration; the mountain of his agony; the mountain of the Cross; and finally, the mountain of the Risen Lord. . . . But in the background we also catch sight of Sinai, Horeb, Moriah—the mountains of Old Testament revelation. They are all at one and the same time mountains of passion and of Revelation, and they also refer in turn to the Temple Mount, where Revelation becomes liturgy. (308–9)

Now follows an exposition of the synoptic stories of the transfiguration (309–13) in which Ratzinger stresses Jesus' unity with the Father and the close connection between the transfiguration and passion accounts. In answer to the earlier question of whether the feast of Tabernacles or Exodus 24 is the background for the transfiguration, Ratzinger equivocates by saying that both matter. For one thing, a connection with the feast of Tabernacles is present because at the time of Jesus this feast had a messianic connotation and because the transfiguration signified the beginning of the messianic era. For another, in Jesus' proclamation as the Son of God to whom the disciples should listen (Mark 9:7), we see a connection with Moses, who on the mountain "received the Torah, God's teaching word" (316).

Ratzinger concludes his discourse with an interpretation of the "obscure statement" in Mark 9:1 that some standing there will not taste death until they see the kingdom of God come in power. Jesus, he proposes, has spoken this word with reference to the three disciples with him and to the transfiguration which takes place immediately afterwards. "On the mountain the three of them see the glory of God's Kingdom shining out of Jesus" (317).

Critique

On p. 309–17: Ratzinger commits a serious error by understanding the transfiguration story as an historical report and concomitantly regarding Jesus' prediction in Mark 9:1 to have been fulfilled by that event. Scholars have long recognized that Mark 9:1 reflects the delay of Jesus' Second Coming; that its apparent oblique reference to the transfiguration event has nothing to do with its original meaning; and that the transfiguration story is a modified and relocated Easter narrative. I add a longer than usual survey at this point because it may serve as an introduction to the real hope of the first Christians:

Mark 9:1

And he [=Jesus] said to them: "Truly, I say to you, there I some standing here who will not taste death before they see that the Kingdom of God has come with power."

Mark has placed this individual saying in the mouth of Jesus and joined it to the previous section by a linking formula ("and he said to them"). Mark, then, is the one who attached the narrative of the transfiguration of Jesus (vv 2–8) to the saying.

The verse relates to the expectation of the end of the world, another term for which is the dawn of the kingdom of God. This expectation is reinterpreted by Mark: with the imminent transfiguration of Jesus the kingdom of God has already come in power and has been seen by the three chief disciples—Peter, James and John.

The saying that Mark has inserted here arose in the time after the death and "resurrection" of Jesus when the expectation of the coming of Jesus from heaven was still alive; the kingdom of God was expected to come in power, and this although some of the disciples had, contrary to expectations, died. This purported saying of Jesus was intended to reassure the disciples who were still alive that at least a small remnant of the first generation will survive to see the dawn of the kingdom of God. Jesus' pronouncement allows them to rely on that.

The letters of Paul, the only eyewitness to have left written accounts of the first Christian generation, give us some insight into the problem of the "delay" of the Second Coming of Jesus. In 1 Cor 15:51 he relates a mystery that he has experienced, i.e. a saying of the Lord granted to him as an apostle to solve the problems in that community:

All of us shall not sleep,
All of us, though, will be changed.

Then follows a description of the end, emphasizing its sudden appearance, laying stress on the trumpet of judgment, and confirming the raising of the dead (1 Cor 15:52).

This saying has to be read against the horizon of the primitive Christian expectation of the imminent end of the world and thus the arrival of the Lord Jesus from Heaven. It alters this expectation to the effect that most will die, but some could count on surviving to the end.

We find a preliminary stage of this changed expectation for the future in Paul's earliest letter, that to the Thessalonians. Here the saying of "the Lord" vouchsafed to the prophet Paul runs as follows:

1 Thessalonians 4:15–17

[15]This we say to you in a word of the Lord, that we who are alive, who are left until the Lord's coming, shall by no means precede those who

have fallen asleep. ¹⁶For the Lord himself will descend from heaven with a cry of command, with the archangel's call, and with the sound of the trumpet of God. And the dead in Christ will rise first; ¹⁷then we who are alive, who are left, shall be caught up together with them in the clouds to meet the Lord in the air; and so we shall always be with the Lord.

When he composed 1 Thessalonians, Paul evidently expected that the majority of Christians, himself included, could reckon on surviving until the advent of Jesus from heaven, whereas a minority would have died.

In short, the origin of the saying in Mark 9:1 demonstrates its non-authenticity. Yet together with the evidence from Paul's letters, of Paul, it makes clear the first generation's ardent expectation of the world's imminent end. And this might in turn be taken to indicate that Jesus himself anticipated the coming of the kingdom of God in the immediate future.

Matthew 10:23
When they persecute you in one town, flee to the next. Truly, I [=Jesus] say to you, you will not have gone through all the towns of Israel before the Son of man comes.

This saying does not fit smoothly in its context—one more reason for regarding it as a saying that was handed down in isolation. Note that Matthew has taken vv 17b–22 from Mark 13:9–12 and vv 24–25 from Q (=Luke 6:40 with parallels in John 13:16; 15:20). He must have come across the present saying and woven it into the gospel in order to intensify Jesus' warning to the disciples about their future destiny (vv 17–25).

The logion reflects a burning expectation of an imminent end. For the person who spoke it and those whom he addressed, it was bound up with the conviction that they would experience the day of the Son of Man in their own lifetimes. This saying dates the anticipated end of the world, for if the disciples will not have to endure persecution for long, then either none or only a minority of them will die. Otherwise this text would have been meaningless, and therefore it must belong to an even earlier time than Mark 9:1, which we have just investigated.

Some scholars regard this saying as authentic because v 23b contains an unfulfilled prediction. But this argument is not convincing, since an early Christian prophet could just as readily have made a prophecy that was not fulfilled. The saying can be readily derived, however, from the situation of the community after the death and "resurrection" of Jesus. Missionaries would have been campaigning in Israel for belief in Christ and would have been exposed to many difficulties. Paul again provides a parallel. He instructs his communities beforehand that they must expect persecution (1 Thess 3:3–4), and that Jesus' Second Coming is imminent (1 Thess 4:15–17).

A further consideration that tells against the authenticity of Matt 10:23 is the lack of any report of widespread or extreme persecution, or fleeing disciples during Jesus' lifetime.

Mark 13:30
Truly, I say to you, this generation will not pass away before all these things take place.

This saying is closely related to the saying in Mark 9:1 (see above, p. 105). And could well have been adapted on that basis by Mark himself for Jesus' discourse on the last things (Mark 13:5–37): Or it could have been inserted here as a saying about the date of the onset of the end. It signals the dying out of the first generation, for apparently the first deaths in the community have led to a modification of the imminent expectation. Although some Christians have died, the first generation will nevertheless witness the coming of the Son of man. The most plausible explanation of the statement that at least some of the first generation will not have to die is that the whole of the first generation were originally expected to experience the end of the age.

The saying thus reflects a delay in the end events; and since Jesus might be seen to have expected the imminent advent of the kingdom of God, the saying in Mark 13:30 is certainly non-authentic.

John 21:22–23
^{22}[Jesus says to Peter about the Beloved Disciple:] "If it is my will that he remain until I come, what is that to you?"

^{23a}The saying spread abroad among the disciples: "This disciple will not die." ^{23b}Yet, Jesus has not said to him: "He will not die," but: "If it is my will that he remain until I come, what is that to you?"

Verse 23a reports the expectation that the Beloved Disciple would not die until the Second Coming of Jesus. Nevertheless he died before Jesus' arrival, and the community therefore devised the following explanation: Jesus had not said that the Beloved Disciple would not die, but had merely asked whether Peter had any right to object to the fulfillment of Jesus' will (vv 22 and 23b). Clearly an error has been corrected by a reinterpretation of a reported saying of Jesus. Verse 22 is not an authentic saying of Jesus. But v 23a, which represents an earlier version of v 22 (now "corrected" by v 23b), is also inauthentic, since the word that is interpreted derives from an early Christian prophet, not from Jesus.

THE BOTTOM LINE: Both the transfiguration story and the passion predictions, which according to the Synoptics Jesus spoke in reaction to Peter's confession, are post-Easter formulations of the Christian community faced with facts that did not mesh with the faith-statements and promises they had been brought up on. As such they contribute nothing to our understanding of the historical Jesus. Clearly, Ratzinger has no stomach for objective textual analysis; in the end his only real concern seems to be providing his readers with a profusion of devout platitudes in the hope that by so doing he may keep them from entertaining any doubts concerning the doctrines of the Church.

Chapter Twelve
on Chapter 10
Jesus Declares His Identity

By transforming an inspiring prophet and teacher into a mythic messiah he never claimed to be, Ratzinger has betrayed not only his readers but his protagonist as well.

This chapter consists of preliminary comments and three subsections, "The Son of Man," "The Son," and "I am."

Overview of pp. 319–21

In his introductory remarks Ratzinger emphasizes that "the only philosophical term that was incorporated into the Creed" is the word *homoousios*, 'of the same substance'" (320; cf. 'consubstantial,' [355]). It "serves . . . to safeguard the reliability of the *biblical* term. It tells us that when Jesus' witnesses call him the 'the Son', this statement is not meant in a mythological or political sense—those being the two most obvious interpretations given the context of the time. Rather, it is meant to be understood quite literally: Yes, in God himself there is an eternal dialogue between Father and Son, who are both truly one and the same God in the Holy Spirit" (320).

Critique

By employing the dichotomy "mythological" vs. "literal" in speaking of God, Ratzinger not only claims a reality for his own version of God, but at the same time, and in a subtle yet ultimately triumphalist way, relegates other individuals' or groups' divinities to the status of myth. The strategy loses its efficacy, however, as the internal mythology of his own "literal" image becomes immediately clear: "[I]n God himself there is an eternal dialogue between Father and Son, who are both truly one and the same God in the Holy Spirit." As he is not allowing these positions to be adopted as metaphor, but rather asserts their literal existence, he has opened his statement up to a scrutiny that can only end in the dissolving of his argument.

Overview of pp. 321–35
The Son of Man

Ratzinger begins his discourse as follows:

> Son of Man—this mysterious term is the title that Jesus most frequently uses to speak of himself. In the Gospel of Mark alone the term occurs fourteen times on Jesus' lips. In fact, in the whole of the New Testament, the term 'Son of Man' is found only on Jesus' lips, with the single exception of the vision of the open heavens that is granted to the dying Stephen: "Behold, I see the heavens opened, and the Son of Man standing at he right hand of God" (Acts 7:56). At the moment of his death, Stephen sees what Jesus had foretold during his trial before the Sanhedrin: "You will see the Son of Man seated at the right hand of the Power, and coming with the clouds of heaven" (Mk 14:62). Stephen is therefore actually 'citing' a saying of Jesus, the truth of which he is privileged to behold at the very moment of his martyrdom. (321–22)

Ratzinger is dissatisfied with the discussion of the Son of Man in current exegesis, for in his view it has left behind "a graveyard of mutually contradictory hypotheses" (322). In general, he says, modern exegetes distinguish three classes of statements: those that concern "the Son of Man who is to come," those dealing with "the earthly activity of the Son of Man," and those that speak "of his suffering and Resurrection" (322–23). They regard as possibly authentic the sayings of the coming Son of Man, whereas the words of the presently active Son of Man and those of the suffering Son of Man are considered non-authentic. To this Ratzinger objects: "Splitting up the Son of Man sayings in this way is the way of a certain kind of logic that meticulously classifies the different aspects of a title. While that might be appropriate for rigorous professorial thinking, it does not suit the complexity of living reality, in which a multilayered whole clamors for expression" (323). This "toned-down" approach, he says, is unable to account for "the powerful impact of the Jesus-event" (324) that led to the crucifixion of Jesus.

At this point Ratzinger offers some historical reflections that supposedly open a way for understanding:

> For such a radical collision to occur, provoking the extreme step of handing Jesus over to the Romans, something dramatic must have been said and done. The great and stirring events come right at the beginning; the nascent Church could only slowly come to appreciate

their full significance, which she came to grasp as, in "remembering" them, she gradually thought through and reflected on these events. The anonymous community is credited with an astonishing level of theological genius—who were the great figures responsible for inventing all this? No, the greatness, the dramatic newness comes directly from Jesus; within the faith and life of the community it is further developed, but not created. In fact, the "community" would not have even emerged and survived at all unless some extraordinary reality had preceded it. (324)

By the term "Son of Man" Jesus has both hidden his mystery and has progressively made it accessible, according to Ratzinger: "In both Hebrew and Aramaic usage, the first meaning of the term 'Son of Man' is simply 'man'. That simple word blends together with a mysterious allusion to a new consciousness of mission in the term 'Son of Man'" (324) which becomes visible in Mark 2:27–28: "The Sabbath was made for man, not man for the Sabbath. So the Son of Man is Lord even over the Sabbath." This means, our author says, "In the Son of Man, man is revealed as he truly ought to be. In terms of the Son of Man, in terms of the criterion that Jesus himself is, man is free and he knows how to use the Sabbath properly as the day of freedom deriving from God and destined for God" (325).

After explaining the occurrence of the term Son of Man in the Old Testament book of Daniel, in 4 Ezra and the Ethiopian book of Enoch (325–27), Ratzinger turns to the three groups of the Son of Man sayings in the New Testament:

1. Those in the first group refer to his future coming and are located mainly in Jesus' discourse about the end of the world (Mark 13:24–27) and his trial before the Sanhedrin (cf. Mark 14:62) (327–28). Ratzinger rejects the view that Luke 12:8–9 and 17:24–25 distinguish between the Son of Man and Jesus. Rather, the two are equated, and thus Jesus identifies himself with the coming Son of Man (cf. Mark 8:38) (329). Indeed, Ratzinger claims, they are "one and the same person . . . the very person, in fact, who, as he speaks these words, is already on the way to his suffering" (330).

Therefore, we are told, the "judges of the Sanhedrin actually understood Jesus properly; he did not correct them by saying something like 'But you misunderstand me; the coming Son of Man is someone else'" (330). Moreover, the inner unity between Jesus' practiced self-humiliation and "his coming in glory is the constant motif of his words and actions; this is what is authentically new about Jesus, it is no invention—on the contrary, it is the epitome of his figure and his words" (330).

2. In the sayings about the present activity of the Son of Man, such as Jesus' assertion of his power to forgive sins in Mark 2:10–11, Ratzinger tells us that "he is claiming to possess the dignity of God himself and to act on that basis" (331).

3. For Ratzinger the sayings of the suffering Son of Man are likewise authentic. "Earlier exegesis considered the blending together of Daniel's vision of the coming Son of Man with the images of the Suffering Servant of God transmitted by Isaiah to be the characteristically new and specific feature of Jesus' idea of the Son of Man—indeed, as the center of his self-understanding overall. It was right to do so" (332). One must take into account, however, that Jesus' image of the Son of Man "brings together even more strands and currents of Old Testament tradition"—such as Psalms 110, 118 and Wisdom of Solomon 2 (332).

In summary, Ratzinger writes: "The enigmatic term 'Son of Man' presents us in a concentrated form with all that is most original and distinctive about the figure of Jesus, his mission, and his being. He comes from God and he is God. But that is precisely what makes him—having assumed human nature—the bringer of true humanity" (333–34).

Critique

On p. 324: To be sure, only dramatic events can account for the rapid growth of Christianity, but it is unlikely that Jesus was himself the primary instigator of the growth—for the simple reason that Gentiles, among whom the religion spread most notably, were not directly addressed by his ministry.[1] Ratzinger overlooks Paul's decisive role in the expansion of Christianity. Indeed, we can observe in his authentic letters[2] that he and the Greek-speaking Jewish Christians whom he had persecuted[3] *did* create new things. Against the bitter opposition of Jesus' own disciples, Paul was instrumental in establishing the equal status of Gentile Christians in the Church.[4] Assuming that the members of the original Twelve had not completely misunderstood their master, Paul's ministry must have been in some ways alien or even antithetical to Jesus' teachings.

While it is true that modern exegesis credits anonymous communities with a high level of theological genius, it is also true that careful analysis of texts that Ratzinger conveniently omits has demonstrated that they were clearly formulated by Christians whose names are not preserved. The last writing of the New Testament, Revelation, provides many examples of the fact that early Christian prophets were in the habit of speaking in the name of the "Risen One" (cf. Rev. 3:20; 16:15), and thus their words were often identified with those of Jesus.

On pp. 323 and 331: Jesus' predictions of his passion—first reported by Mark and subsequently appropriated by the other synoptic writers—are not authentic. A brief exposition of the passages at hand should place this point beyond question.

Mark 8:31

And he began to teach them: "The Son of Man must suffer many things, and be rejected by the elders and the chief priests and the scribes, and be killed, and after three days rise."

Mark 9:31

He was teaching his disciples and saying to them: "The Son of Man will be delivered into the hands of men, and they will kill him, and when he is killed, after three days he will rise."

Mark 10:32b–34

[32b]And taking the Twelve again, he began to tell them what was to happen to him: [33]"Look, we are going up to Jerusalem; and the Son of Man will be delivered to the chief priests and scribes. And they will condemn him to death, and deliver him to the Gentiles [34]and they will mock him, and spit on him, and scourge him, and kill him; after three days he will rise."

The first prediction of the passion and resurrection (Mark 8:31) seems to be the basis for the second and third predictions of the passion and resurrection. Mark may have received it from tradition and has given the third prediction special weight by adding details that conform to his passion account. Note that three key verbs used here also appear in the passion narrative: "condemn" (cf. 14:64), "mock" (cf. 15:20, 31), "spit on" (cf. 14:65; 15:19). For "scourge," see 15:15.

By means of these three announcements of the passion (and especially the third), Mark indicates that Jesus is going voluntarily to Jerusalem to die there; for this is both necessary and in accordance with the will of the Father (cf. 8:31a). Jesus predicts his end right down to the gruesome details, yet will not be diverted from his decision.

No doubt Mark had a didactic purpose as well, for if Jesus knew of his death and resurrection in advance and predicted it, he must really be the Lord of life and death.[5] We see the completion of this development in John 10:17–18: [17]"For this reason the Father loves me, because I lay down my life, that I may take it again. [18]No one takes it from me, but I lay it down on my own accord. I have power to lay it down, and I have power to take it again. This charge I have received from my Father."

By linking the third prediction of the passion so closely with the passion narrative, Mark adds an anti-Jewish feature (see also Matt 21:33–46; 22:1–14; 23:13–28 and John 8:37–45). For the killing of Jesus accomplishes the plan the Jewish authorities have been cherishing since the beginning of Jesus' public ministry: "The Pharisees went out, and immediately held counsel with the Herodians against him, how to destroy him" (Mark 3:6).

The evangelist's clear intent in the *threefold* prediction of the passion and resurrection tells decisively against its historicity.

In fact, attempts to defend the historicity of even the *first* prediction (Mark 8:31) are doomed to failure. For one thing, its undisguised anti-Judaism does not sit well on the lips of a devoted Jew. For another, it is not credible that Jesus spoke of his resurrection after three days, for the hasty flight of the disciples (Mark 14:50) after Jesus' arrest indicates that they had no such hope. Therefore, Jesus' prediction of his own resurrection must have been assigned to him at a later stage in the development of the story. In short, the reported predictions have no reasonable claim to authenticity.

Overview of pp. 335–45
The Son

At the beginning of this section Ratzinger discusses the historical background of the title "Son of God" (335–37), and concerning Acts 13:32–33 writes that the early Christians considered the resurrection of Jesus the fulfillment of God's word in Ps 2:7: "You are my son, today I have begotten you" (338). In the first century, then, two assertions stand in direct conflict: "the Roman emperor's claim to divine kingship encounters the Christian belief that the risen Christ is the true Son of God, the Lord of all the peoples of the earth, to whom alone belongs worship in the unity of the Father, Son, and Spirit" (339). The term "Son of God" must be distinguished from "'the Son,' which essentially we find only on the lips of Jesus" (339) The term appears most often in the Fourth Gospel, but also in the "joyful shout" in Matt 11:25–27/Luke 10:21–22. This exclamation reflects Jesus' ontological oneness with God, the unity of will between Father and Son, and God's desire to draw those who are pure in heart into the Son's filial knowledge (340–43).

The term "the Son" corresponds to the simple address "Abba" whose real origin lies in Jesus' prayer. "Joachim Jeremias has devoted a number of in-depth-studies to demonstrating the uniqueness of this form of address that Jesus used for God, since it implied an intimacy that was impossible in the world of his time. It expresses the 'unicity' of the 'Son'" (344). Indeed, the term "Abba" as well as the corresponding "Son" allows us to look into both the inner side of Jesus and of God. "We have to reckon with the originality of Jesus. Only he is 'the Son'" (345).

Critique

On pp. 344–45: In his address of God as "Abba" Jesus hardly differs from other Jews.[6] Therefore it is incorrect to say that this address was unimaginable in Jesus' world. For the Jews, God was always, among other things, father. The book of Sirach alone has three examples of the appeal to God the Father: "one in Greek, 'O Lord, Father and Ruler of my life' (23.1); one in Hebrew, 'I will praise you, O my God, my salvation, I will thank you my God, my Father' (51.1), and one in both languages, 'I exalted the Lord: you are my Father' (51.10)."[7] An identity of "substance" between God himself and one who addresses him as Father simply does not admit of empirical ascertainment. Ratzinger both overreaches himself and offends against rational discourse when he reads the *homoousia* of later church dogmatics into Jesus' address to God.

Overview of pp. 345–55

I am

Ratzinger now launches into a discussion of the formula "I am" by focusing on two passages in the Fourth Gospel and a synoptic parallel, Mark 6:50.

An important instance of this formula, he says, is in John 8:24: "You will die in your sins unless you believe that I am he." On one hand the spiritual root of this word lies in Exodus 3:14 where God from the burning bush tells Moses his name, YHWH, and later gives its meaning thus: "I am who I am" (Exod 3:14). Isa 43:10–11 ("that you may know and believe me and understand that I am he") provides an even clearer and more emphatic context (346–47).

When Jesus says, "I am he," he is taking up the story of the burning bush and referring it "to himself. He is indicating his oneness. In him the mystery of the one God is personally present: 'I and the Father are one'" (348).

After that Ratzinger turns to John 8:28 ("When you have lifted up the Son of Man, then you will know that I am he") and explains that on the cross the oneness of Jesus with the Father becomes visible. Even more, the "burning bush is the Cross. The highest claim of revelation, the 'I am he,' and the Cross of Jesus are inseparably one. What we find here is not metaphysical speculation, but the self-revelation of God's reality in the midst of history for us" (349).

On John 8:58 ("Before Abraham came into existence, I am") Ratzinger opines thus: "Jesus' 'I am' stands in contrast to the world of birth and death, the world of coming into being and passing away" (350).

Thus in the story of Jesus' walking on the water (Mark 6:45–51; cf. John 6:16–21) the phrase "I am he" is not "a simple identifying formula by means of which Jesus enables his followers to recognize him" (351). Since the disciples' fear subsequently increases, one must conclude that "The Jesus who walks upon the waters is not simply the familiar Jesus; in this new Jesus they suddenly recognize the presence of God himself" (352). Likewise the calming of the storm by Jesus is "an act that exceeds the limits of man's abilities and indicates the power of God at work" (352)

Now Ratzinger turns to the seven "I-am-Sayings" of the Fourth Gospel "in which the 'I am' is given a specific content by the use of some image" (352). The common meaning of these sayings—"I am the bread of life," "I am the light of the world," etc.[8]—is that Jesus has come to give life to human beings. "In the end, man needs just one thing. . . . He needs God. . . . Jesus gives us 'life' because he gives us God. He can give God because he himself is one with God" (353–54).

In summary, Ratzinger concludes,

> We have found three terms in which Jesus at once conceals and reveals the mystery of his person: "Son of Man," "Son," "I am he." All three of these terms demonstrate how deeply rooted he is in the Word of God, Israel's Bible, the Old Testament. And yet all these terms receive their full meaning only in him; it is as if they had been waiting for him. . . . All three are therefore possible only on his lips. . . . None of the three terms as such could therefore be straightforwardly adopted as a confessional statement by the 'community,' by the Church in its early stages of formation." (354)

Therefore, the early Christians adopted the phrase "Son of God," which acquired a wholly new meaning.

On this basis Ratzinger again defends the use of the word *homoousios* ("consubstantial"—earlier [320] translated by "of the same substance"). This term did not hellenize the faith, he assures us, but "captured in a stable formula exactly what had emerged as incomparably new and different in Jesus' way of speaking with the Father" (355).

Critique

On pp. 345–55: Ratzinger regards the formula "I am he" as an authentic word of Jesus and as a hint that Jesus has thought of himself to be of the same substance as God. Yet, for one thing the fact that these sayings occur almost only in the Fourth Gospel speaks against the authenticity of this formula—despite Ratzinger's futile attempt to trace it back to an eyewitness. For another, a number of clearly historical actions and sayings exclude the historicity of the claim that lies behind the formula. Let me mention only Jesus' decision to be baptized for the forgiveness of sins (see above, pp. 20–22) and his answer to a man who addresses him as "good teacher" that "nobody is good except for God alone" (Mark 10:18). Somebody who considers himself an equal to God would hardly behave or speak in such ways.

On p. 349: When Ratzinger says that the burning bush and the cross are "inseparably one," he is indulging himself in figurative discourse. In an appropriate context that might be all very well, but in a book purporting to deal with the historical Jesus it is utterly inadmissible. When he then says that this flight of fancy is "not metaphorical speculation, but the self-revelation of God's reality," he becomes ridiculous.

On pp. 351–52: Ratzinger considers the episode reported in Mark 6:45–51 as factual and derives from it Jesus' self-understanding to be like God. He thereby loses any remaining claim to credibility, for the historicity of such an unbelievable legend simply cannot be defended, as the following brief exegesis will show:

Mark 6:45–51

Jesus walks on the sea

⁴⁵And immediately he urged his disciples to get into the boat and go before him to the other shore to Bethsaida, while he himself dismissed the people. ⁴⁶And he took his leave of them and went up to the mountain to pray.

⁴⁷And when evening had come, the boat was in the middle of the sea and he was alone on the land. ⁴⁸And he saw them toiling away at the oars, for the wind was against them, and in the fourth watch of the night he comes to them walking on the sea. And he wanted to pass by them. ⁴⁹But when they saw him walking on the sea, they thought that it was a ghost and they cried out. ⁵⁰For they saw him and were perplexed. But he immediately spoke with them and said to them: "Take courage, it is I, do not fear!" ⁵¹And he went to them into the boat and the wind died down.

Classification in terms of form shows this passage to be an epiphany story, and thus different from the saving miracle in Mark 4:35–41 (Jesus' earlier calming of the waves). However, it is sometimes asked whether the two are not variants of one and the same archetypal narrative. If that were the case, the stilling of the storm (vv 48, 51) must have been the original motif, now forced into the background by the miracle of walking on water. But the abrupt statement in v 48 ("He wanted to pass by them") shows that in the tradition, the walking on the sea stood at the beginning.

Jesus' walking on the sea is meant to show his superiority (or at least equality) to other sons of god in the first-century religious environment for whom similar claims were made. For in antiquity the ability to walk on water was regarded as a divine power. Old Testament parallels are also to be noted here, according to which God can walk on the water or on the waves of the sea (see Job 9:8; Ps 77:20).

The story of Jesus walking on the sea may derive from an Easter story (cf. John 21). Verses 49–50 would nicely suit that context: Jesus' presence is emphasized and the disciples' fear that they have seen a ghost is rejected (cf. Luke 24:36–43 in the framework of an Easter story). At a second stage such an Easter narrative could appropriately have been expended into a miracle of rescue from distress at sea.

What all of these examples have in common, however, is not the faintest claim to or proof of historicity, but rather an allegorical attempt at bolstering faith. They cannot be used by anyone, including Ratzinger, to assert an empirical reality or—specifically here—an attribute of the historical Jesus.

THE BOTTOM LINE: Jesus, a Jew from Galilee, prayed to the God of the Bible of Israel. He did not place himself on God's level, which would have been blasphemy. His historical followers could not have witnessed events such as the miracle-myths Ratzinger dwells on in his "scholarly" exposition. Their following was based on other ideas of a more earthly—but no less inspiring—nature. Ratzinger's emphasis on the supernatural and the theological hierarchy of and in the New Testament has produced a lamentable result for lay and academic readers alike. He has wrested the charismatic, complex Jesus, Galilean teacher of righteousness, from his actual historical context and thrust him center-stage into a mythological drama not of his invention.

Epilogue
Ten Objections to Joseph Ratzinger's Book on Jesus

1. Ratzinger both labels and describes his work inaccurately, if not deceptively. The intent suggested by his title and announced in his preface, namely to discover by means of the gospels the historical Jesus, is in fact not carried out. Moreover, far from addressing mere historical issues, the book is replete with doctrinally based arguments and personal meditations on his Lord. Thus, the actual subject is not the Jesus of history, but rather the Christ of faith.

2. Although the Gospel of John is often invoked in the book, this last of the four accounts of the life of Jesus offers little of historical value. The long-standing scholarly view is that since its motives and social concerns reflect the contemporary community of its author, any claim to historicity is highly questionable. Furthermore, the same general assessment applies to the Synoptics; for despite numerous textual and narrative concurrences, each can be shown to be a product of its own historical context. Thus the primary resemblance of the three earlier gospels to the fourth is that none of them constitutes an eyewitness account of events.

3. Historical research into the composition of the gospels receives at best short shrift and at worst a peremptory dismissal by the Pope. The "Two-Document" hypothesis, according to which Matthew and Luke independently used Mark and the Sayings Gospel Q as source-material, forms the commonly accepted basis of both modern investigation of the gospels and of historical-Jesus research. Ratzinger arbitrarily repudiates this scholarly consensus insisting on the historical accuracy of the gospels. The effect of this unilateral dismissal is to raise the question of the true nature of Ratzinger's endeavor; and to suggest that his purpose is to reinstate pre-critical exegetical scholarship.

4. Ratzinger's criticisms of both contemporary studies of the historical Jesus and earlier scholars whose opinions differ from his are founded not on substantiated research but on faith-based accep-

tance. Although he claims to offer a reasoned assessment of the Jesus implicit in the gospel accounts, his book fails to display the critical integrity and intellectual honesty characteristic of both liberal Protestant and modernist Catholic theologians.

5. The accepted tenets of historical reasoning thus reveal the inadequacy of Ratzinger's interpretations. Moreover, by using historical-critical language to strengthen his theologically based understanding, he abuses the very methodology he claims to be adopting. His Jesus is not the first-century Galilean of that name, but a creature of his own, doctrinally driven imagination. Ratzinger's interpretations therefore violate the accepted tenets of historical reasoning. Worse yet, he violates the very methodology he claims to embrace by employing historical-critical language to promote purely theological assertions. The Jesus he offers us is therefore not the first-century Galilean teacher who bore that name, but the creation of a doctrinally driven imagination.

6. Ratzinger displays an unfortunate habit of many earlier biblical interpreters when he evokes numerous elements of the "Old Testament" as predictive revelations of Christ. This anachronism is of course scientifically impermissible—but does conform to his doctrinal view very nicely. Moreover, the irresponsible insistence upon the term "Old Testament" in referring to the Hebrew Bible reflects both a lack of sensitivity for present-day Jewish communities, whose identity is rooted in these writings, and a regressive approach to Christian-Jewish relations.

7. As a lifelong and pious Jew, Jesus of Nazareth never stated and certainly did not consider himself to be divine or one with the Deity. Only with the rise of Gentile Christianity near the beginning of the second century did Jesus come to be widely regarded as God. To suggest otherwise demonstrates unfamiliarity with the texts in question and a preponderant concern with indoctrination rather than history.

8. The many contradictions between the images of Jesus in the four gospels are partly due to the fact that Jesus did not utter most of the words attributed to him by the Evangelists, each of whom was speaking to and for a particular community. Thus, it behooves responsible scholarship to distinguish between authentic and inauthentic sayings and actions of Jesus as the first step in any reasonable study of Jesus.

9. Understanding the biblical texts on the basis of their supposed divine inspiration can never be squared with the human search for objective truth. Whoever has given a little finger to the historical-critical method must give the whole hand.

10. In the real world, when faith and knowledge stand in contradiction, the latter should have priority. That the historical-critical method has produced conflicting images of Jesus is not an argument against it; rather, these findings, however nettlesome to absolutists, should encourage critical scholars to improve upon the work of their predecessors. Historical criticism is constantly correcting itself; it is never content to repeat with self-congratulatory certainty the subsequently disproven speculations of past ages.

Notes

Prologue

1. Harvey, *The Historian and the Believer*, 42.
2. Ratzinger, *Jesus of Nazareth*. References to this book are given in parentheses.

Chapter 1

1. Among others, Ratzinger cites Guardini, whose book, *The Humanity of Christ*, he subsequently evaluates positively (see chap. 5, note 1). On the concept of theology as a science, Guardini offers the following definitive statement: "Science is the study of a subject by means of the method required by this subject, not by means of some generally applicable method which undermines its specific character. Theology can be called a science precisely because it uses, not the methods of general history or psychology, but the method demanded by the nature of the object being investigated, which in this case is revelation. . . . Theology is rigorously scientific only when it accepts the nature of revelation as the determining factor in its choice of method" (*The Humanity of Christ*, xix–xx n. 1).
2. Schnackenburg, *Jesus in the Gospels*, 316—summarizing the first chapter of his book (1–16), which has the title "Faith and History."
3. "And he has become flesh."
4. See Childs, *Biblical Theology*. In general, Childs and his followers neglect historical questions and never reach a level beyond Sunday school lectures.
5. But of course it does. For example, it is clear that the beginning and ending sections of Ecclesiastes deprive the original document of any claim to original historical unity.
6. Troeltsch, "On Historical and Dogmatic Method in Theology," 740–41 (my translation).
7. Here and in the following I am using Matthew, Mark, Luke, and John as the names of the authors of the four gospels though their real names remain unknown.
8. This preface most likely included Acts (cf. Acts 1:1).

Chapter 2

1. "No one has ever seen God; it is the only Son, who is nearest to the Father's heart, who has made him known."
2. On Harnack see further my pp. 34–38.
3. Concerning the Fourth Gospel's supposedly eyewitness reports to the effect of Jesus' assertions of a direct relationship with the Deity, see my pp. 79–85.
4. The "historical method" used by Ratzinger has the sole aim of proving the reliability of the Gospels; in fact, however, he never examines their historical trustworthiness, as we discover repeatedly in reading his book. Incidentally,

this is a wise strategy on his part. "The historical method, once it is applied to biblical scholarship and church history, is a leaven which transforms everything and which finally causes the form of all previous theological methods to disintegrate. . . . Give historical method your little finger and it will take your whole hand" (Troeltsch, "On Historical and Dogmatic Method in Theology," 730, 734 [my translation]).

Chapter 3

1. Such a consideration of "novelty," however, flies directly in the face of any claim to historical veracity. For surely the only thing "new" to those present at the event would have been the Baptist's announcement of the approaching personage. This announcement may have taken place in fact, but its metaphysical nature immediately situates the entire happening in the realm of the incredible or non-factual.

2. As a personal aside here, I find it difficult to understand how the supreme head of the Roman Catholic Church—and an educated scholar—would continue to insist upon such superficial interpretation and imagery some 400 years after Galileo and 300 years after Newton.

3. The population of Jerusalem at the time of Jesus was about 25,000 inhabitants. See Jeremias, *Jerusalem at the Time of Jesus*, 84.

4. Cf. Luke 3:7–9: [7]"You brood of vipers, who has assured you that you will escape the future wrath? [8]See that you bear righteous fruits of repentance, and do not begin to say to yourselves, 'We have Abraham as our Father.' For I say to you, God can raise up children to Abraham from these stones. [9]Already the axe is laid to the roots of the trees; every tree that does that does not bear good fruit will be cut down and thrown into fire."

5. Cf. 2 Cor 5:21; John 8:46; 1 John 3:5; 1 Pet 2:22; Heb 4:15. According to the Gospel of the Nazoreans, (not included in the canon), Jesus expressly refused baptism from John: "How have I sinned? So why I should go and get baptized by him?" (Translation following Miller, *Complete Gospels*, 443.) But of course it is not in Ratzinger's plan, or perhaps interest, to bring in any materials other than the canonical.

6. John 3:22–23; 4:1 (but note the correction in John 4:2: "Although Jesus himself did not baptize, but his disciples;" see also 1:33).

7. Matt 3:15; 5:6, 10, 20; 6:1, 33; 21:32.

8. Strecker, *Sermon on the Mount*, 37.

9. Cf. Luke 5:16; 6:12; 9:18; 11:1.

Chapter 4

1. Notice how Ratzinger works on the level of image—moving from one to another like one walking on ice floes.

2. Cf. Geering, *Christianity Without God*, in which he goes so far as to propose that "the modern secular world has evolved . . . as the natural result of taking the doctrine of the incarnation to its logical conclusion" (132). Indeed, secular humanists also have their "Saints" such as Sebastian Franck (1499–1542), Sebastian Castellio (1515–1563), and Gotthold Ephraim Lessing (1729–1781). Without their lifelong efforts religious freedom might still be denied to us as it long was to much of the world and still is to millions.

3. Cf. further Bartimäus (Mark 10:46); Barnabas (Acts 4:36); Barsabbas (Acts 1:23; 15:22).

Chapter 5

1. "Catholic modernism" is a collective label for those groups who, from 1893 to 1914, were involved in a controversy with the Roman Curia over biblical criticism in France. Climactic events included placing Loisy's works on the Index, in 1903, and his excommunication in 1908. For a thorough treatment of these matters, see Bernard B. Scott, "Introduction" to *The Gospel and the Church*, by Alfred Loisy (Philadelphia: Fortress Press, 1976), xv-xxxvii. One of Ratzinger's authorities, Romano Guardini (see above, note 1, chap. 1), delivers a palpable thrust to Catholic modernism in his *The Humanity of Christ*, xv: "How little justice was done to the figure of Christ by the historical and psychological method of the liberal school of theologians! The repercussions of this tendency in Catholicism, known as Modernism, have been overcome. We know not only that a watered-down version of Christianity is erroneous, but also that it is not even worthwhile wasting energy trying to provide it with an intellectual basis. The self-commitment of faith only makes sense when directed towards the one complete, unadulterated revelation with its supra-rational appeal." Guardini seems to look at the issue not from the standpoint of truth but from that of tactics. Moreover, he neglects to mention that modernism was "overcome" by force rather than argument.

2. Ratzinger in fact supplies this quotation in his book (48). The correct citation from Loisy is: "Jesus foretold the kingdom, and it was the Church that came." See my p. 38.

3. It is perhaps significant to indicate here that the man did not in fact "give away" all his possessions but "sold all that he had and bought it [=the precious pearl]" (Matt 13:46).

4. Cf . Mark 1:1, 14, 15; 8:35; 10:29; 13:10; 14:9.

5. Cf. Rom 1:3–4. This text derives from a pre-Pauline creedal formula.

6. Note that in contrast to the Emperor cult "the early Christian preaching employs the term 'Gospel' only in the singular" (Lohse, *Freude des Glaubens*, 16).

7. Loisy, *The Gospel and the Church*, 166.

8. Harnack, *What is Christianity?* Loisy's book was openly intended as a direct answer to Harnack and sought to defend Catholicism against Protestant critics.

9. Loisy, *The Gospel and the Church*, 166.

10. Note also the interpretation of this parable that follows in Matt 13:37b–43.

11. On Luke 10:18 as a genuine word of Jesus, see my p. 66.

12. On the expectation of John the Baptist, see Luke 3:7–9 (my note 4, chap. 3), on that of Paul, see 1 Thess 4:15–17 (my pp. 105–6).

13. Note further that the text includes no "Christian" criterion for acceptance at the last day, and therefore has an authentic — that is, non-post-Easter-ring to it.

14. Ratzinger's approving citation of Luke 17:20–21 gravely undermines him at this point. Whether God's kingdom is "in the midst of you," "among you," or "within you" — the main point is that "the rule of God cannot be empirically observed" (Funk/Hoover, *The Five Gospels*, 365). Since Jesus is standing in full view of his auditors, it is difficult to imagine how he could have considered himself identical with that invisible reality.

Chapter 6

1. Cf. Schäfer, "Die Torah der messianischen Zeit."

2. One problem with this assertion, among many, is that two verses are of dubious authenticity; thus Jesus' intention, or the intention of another, later

writer, whose context is undetermined, is unclear—and certainly cannot be unequivocally seen as responding in some way to the Ten Commandments. See on this Funk/Hoover, *The Five Gospels,* 140, and my pp. 48–49.

3. Cf. 1 Cor 4:9–13; 2 Cor 4:8–10, 4:11, and 6:8–10.

4. This presentation of the great pagan philosopher as a proto-Christian should not go unnoticed—either for its boldness or its implausibility. Space forbids further analysis of the comparison, unfortunately.

5. A similar construction is found in Luke 16:17.

6. After "seeing" the risen Jesus in a revelation near Damascus he went to Arabia and after that returned to Damascus. Only after three years he went to Jerusalem to become acquainted with Cephas (Gal 1:17–18).

7. Neusner, *A Rabbi Talks with Jesus,* 68–69.

8. *A Rabbi Talks with Jesus,* 72.

9. *A Rabbi Talks with Jesus,* 53.

10. Of course, this in effect argues that a long-sustained claim to be free of the strictures of the Jewish Law can be taken as proof of Jesus' divinity. Once again "faith" trumps logic.

11. An example of apodictic law: "Whoever curses his father or his mother shall be put to death" (Exod 21:17); an example of casuistic law: [18]"When men quarrel and one strikes the other with a stone or with his fist and the man does not die but keeps his bed, [19]then if the man rises again and walks abroad with his staff, he that struck him shall be clear; only shall he pay for the loss of his time, and shall have him thoroughly healed" (Exod 21:18–19).

12. The six antitheses (Matt 5:21–48) are of varying lengths and address traditional and "new" views on killing, adultery, divorce, swearing, non-violence, and love of enemy.

13. See Lohse, "Ich aber sage euch."

14. Neusner, *A Rabbi Talks with Jesus,* 145.

15. Cf. *A Rabbi Talks with Jesus,* 16: "This is a book about faith meeting faith."

16. Regardless of whether this practice reflects proper scruples on a scholarly level, it demonstrates a certain lack of respect for Neusner's text itself, as is the case in any inaccurate if not wanton appropriation of one author's ideas to serve another's.

17. Neusner, *A Rabbi Talks with Jesus,* 147.

Chapter 7

1. At this point of course we note that all historical exegesis has been left far behind.

2. John 4:34; Heb 10:5–7; and by analogy, and by anachronistic inference Ps 40:7–9. This line of argument, together with the previous assertion that God has uttered words in history, shows clearly that Ratzinger has chosen to disregard the historical reasoning that he claimed to employ in his book.

3. Cf. Matt 6:25–33/Luke 12:22–31; Luke 10,4.

Chapter 8

1. "And no one who has drunk old (wine) will want new, for he thinks, 'The old one tastes better.'"

2. Cf. John 12:31; Rev 12:7.

3. Worth noting in this context as well is the fact that, at the time of Jesus, the overcoming of Satan in the *future* was expected. Thus where Jesus deviates

from this Jewish tradition is in his presenting a vanquished Satan within his own lifetime. Note, for example, *Ascension of Moses* 10:1: "And then God's rule will appear over his whole creation, and then Satan will be no more, and sorrow will be removed with him."

4. In Greek, *dianoichthêti*.
5. Cf. Mark 1:44–45; 5:43a.
6. Cf. Mark 4:41; 5.7; 6:3.14b.15.50.
7. Cf. Mark 6:7.
8. That is, "Luke" omits the scourging-scene (Mark 15:16–20), so that it is the Jews, rather than Pilate and the Romans, who sanction and thus effect the execution of Jesus (Luke 23:33).
9. Among the more significant citations on this matter we may cite Acts 2:23 and 3:15.
10. See, among other citations, Acts 13:46; 18, etc.
11. Acts 28:26–27.
12. Acts 28:28.

Chapter 9

1. Cited by Jeremias, *Parables of Jesus*, 21. It is a weak argument, as it excludes the possibility of a misunderstanding or a contradiction of Jesus.
2. *Parables of Jesus*, 230.
3. *Parables of Jesus*, 17. I have corrected the English translation at two places on the basis of the German original; see Jeremias, *Gleichnisse Jesu*, 13–14.
4. He further obscures the situation by failing to note that historical-critical work on the Bible, including careful analysis of Jesus' parables, has solved more problems and produced more new insights and understanding than any theological method is able to.
5. Jeremias, *Parables of Jesus*, 17.
6. In the first, an estate manager who has been fired for theft seeks to assure his survival by further swindling his master—who surprisingly commends him for his prudent action. An interesting ambiguity further complicates the situation, for the master who thus approves of the fraud is called *kyrios*, the same word used elsewhere to identify Jesus as "Lord." In the second, the Kingdom of Heaven is compared to a bit of leaven that is hidden in a bushel of flour and turns it all into dough. This is a truly disturbing image, inasmuch as leaven is a repeated symbol of impurity or corruption (see Exod 12:15; Hos 7:4; Matt 16:6; Luke 12:1; 1 Cor 5:7; Gal 5:9), and a bushel (three measures, or one *ephah*) is associated with God's presence in three important passages in the Hebrew Bible (see Gen 18:6; Judg 6:19; 1 Sam 1:24). Attempting to allegorize these narratives would be at best perilous; seeking to assign them christological significance would no doubt be blasphemous.
7. Cf. Acts 4:11; 1 Pet 2:4.6–8.

Chapter 10

1. Bultmann, *The Gospel of John*, 26.
2. Hengel, *The Son of God*, 33.
3. Hengel, *The Johannine Question*, 124–35.
4. Hengel, *The Johannine Question*, 132.
5. Broer, *Einleitung in das Neue Testament*, 197.
6. Hengel, *The Johannine Question*, 132.

7. Cf. Luke 2:19; 2:51.
8. Cf. only John 5,18; 8:12, 14, 19; 23–24, 44–45, 51. See further Strecker, *Theology of the New Testament*, 490–96.
9. Rech, *Inbild des Kosmos*, 303. Theotokos = God-bearer, a title of Mary, the mother of Jesus.
10. The evangelist intends this to refer to Christ; in the putative scriptural sources, the referent is God.
11. Whether this indulgence implicitly justifies other endeavors not expressly prohibited, we are not told.
12. See Funk/Hoover, *The Five Gospels*, 510.
13. Matt 14:13–21; 15:32–48; Mark 6:32–44; 8:1–9; Luke 9:10b–17.
14. "I will put my words in his mouth, and he shall speak to them all that I commanded him."
15. Schönborn, *Weihnacht*, 23–24.
16. Mark 6:30–44; 8:1–10; Matt 14:13–21; 15:32–39; Luke 9:10–17.
17. Elliger, *Buch der zwölf Kleinen Propheten*, 172.

Chapter 11

1. The complete title for this section is: "Two Milestones on Jesus' Way: Peter's Confession and the Transfiguration." It is abbreviated here for the sake of convenience; and the arguments brought forward concern the latter half of the heading alone.
2. This is a logical ruse. He is begging the historical question.
3. "Again the high priest asked him and said to him: 'Are you the Christ, the son of the Most Blessed?' And Jesus said: 'I am, and you will see the Son of man sitting at the right hand of the Power and coming with the clouds of heaven'."
4. Cf. John 1:42
5. Cf. John 11:27.
6. Cf. John 5:18; 10:30.
7. Cf. John 6:30, 36.
8. Cf. Luke 24:11, 37–38, 41; Matt 28:17.
9. Dauer, *Johannes und Lukas*, 253.
10. Cf. 1 John 1:1; 4:1–2; 2 John 7; see also Luke 24:39–43.

Chapter 12

1. Cf. Mark 7:24–30.
2. Rom;1 Cor; 2 Cor; Phil; Gal; 1 Thess; Phlm.
3. Gal 1:23.
4. Gal 2.
5. There is still another factor—the heroic figure of the Jewish martyr.
6. Vermes, *The Religion of Jesus the Jew*, 179 refers to a report (bTaan 23b) about the charismatic rain-maker, Hanan, the grandson of Honi, who had lived at the time of Jesus: "When the world was in need of rain, our rabbis used to send school-children to him (Hanan) who seized the train of his cloak and said: 'Abba, Abba, give us rain!' He said to him (God): 'Lord of the world, do something for those who cannot distinguish between the Abba who gives rain and the Abba who does not give rain.'"
7. Vermes, *The Religion of Jesus the Jew*, 175–76.
8. Cf. John 6:35 ("bread of life"); 8:12 ("light of the world"); 10:9 ("door"); 10:11 ("good shepherd"); 11:25 ("resurrection and life"); 14:6 ("way; truth, life");

# Works Consulted

Broer, Ingo. *Einleitung in das Neue Testament*. Vol 1. Würzburg: Echter, 1998.

Bultmann, Rudolf. *The Gospel of John: A Commentary*. Trans. G. R. Beasley-Murray. Oxford: Blackwell, 1971.

Cazelles, Henri. "Johannes. Ein Sohn des Zebedäus. 'Priester' und Apostel." *Internationale Katholische Zeitschrift Communio* 31 (2002) 479–84.

Childs, Brevard. *Biblical Theology of the Old and New Testaments: Theological Reflection on the Christian Bible*. Minneapolis: Fortress Press, 1993.

Dauer, Anton. *Johannes und Lukas. Untersuchungen zu den johanneisch-lukanischen Parallelperikopen*. Würzburg: Echter Verlag 1984.

Elliger, Karl. *Das Buch der zwölf Kleinen Propheten*. Vol 2. Göttingen: Vandenhoeck & Ruprecht, 1964.

Funk, Robert W. and Roy W. Hoover. *The Five Gospels*. New York: Macmillan, 1993.

Geering Lloyd. *Christianity Without God*. Santa Rosa, CA: Polebridge Press, 2002.

Guardini, Romano. *The Humanity of Christ: Contributions to a Psychology of Jesus*. Trans. Ronald Walls. New York: Random House, 1964.

Harnack, Adolf. *What is Christianity? Lectures Delivered in the University of Berlin During the Winter Term 1899–1900*. Trans. Thomas Bailey Saunders. London: Williams and Norgate, 1901.

Harvey, Van A. *The Historian and the Believer: The Morality of Historical Knowledge and Christian Belief. With a New Introduction by the Author.* Urbana and Chicago: University of Illinois Press, 1996.

Hengel, Martin. *The Son of God: the Origin of Christology and the History of Jewish-Hellenistic Religion*. Trans. John Bowden. Philadelphia: Fortress Press, 1976.

Hengel, Martin. *The Johannine Question*. Trans. John Bowden. Philadephia: Trinity Press International, 1989.

Jeremias, Joachim. *Jerusalem at the Time of Jesus*. Trans. F.H. and C.H. Cave. Philadelphia: Fortress Press, 1969.

Jeremias, Joachim. *Die Gleichnsse Jesu*. 7th ed. Göttingen: Vandenhoeck & Ruprecht, 1965.

Jeremias, Joachim. *The Parables of Jesus*. Trans. S.H. Hooke. Rev. ed. New York: Scribner's Sons, 1972.

Lohse, Eduard. "'Ich aber sage euch.'" Pp. 189–203 in *Der Ruf Jesu und die Antwort der Gemeinde. Exegetische Untersuchungen Joachim Jeremias zum 70. Geburtstag gewidmet von seinen Schülern*. Göttingen: Vandenhoeck and Ruprecht, 1970.

Lohse, Eduard. *Freude des Glaubens. Die Freude im Neuen Testament*. Göttingen: Vandenhoeck & Ruprecht, 2006.

Loisy, Alfred. *The Gospel and the Church. Introduction by Bernard B. Scott*. Philadelphia: Fortress Press, 1976.

Lüdemann, Gerd. *Jesus After Two Thousand Years: What He Really Said and Did*. Trans. John Bowden. Amherst, N.Y.: Prometheus Books, 2001.

Lüdemann, Gerd. *Paul: The Founder of Christianity*. Amherst, N.Y.: Prometheus Books, 2002.

Miller, Robert J., ed. *The Complete Gospels: Annotated Scholars Version*. Rev. and expanded ed. Sonoma, CA: Polebridge Press, 1994.

Neusner, Jacob. *A Rabbi Talks with Jesus*. New York: Doubleday, 1993.

Ratzinger, Joseph—Pope Benedict XVI: *Jesus of Nazareth: From the Baptism in the Jordan to the Transfiguration*. Trans. Adrian J. Walker. New York: Doubleday, 2007.

Rech, Photina. *Inbild des Kosmos. Eine Symbolik der Schöpfung*. Vol 2. Salzburg: Otto Müller, 1966.

Schäfer, Peter. "Die Torah der messianischen Zeit," Pp. 198–213 in id. *Studien zur Geschichte und Theologie des rabbinischen Judentums*. Leiden: Brill, 1978.

Schnackenburg, Rudolf. *Jesus in the Gospels: A Biblical Christology*. Trans. O. C. Dean, Jr. Louisville: Westminster John Knox Press, 1995.

Schönborn, Christoph. *Weihnacht—Mythos wird Wirklichkeit. Meditationen zur Menschwerdung Jesu*. 2d ed., Einsiedeln, 1992.

Strecker, Georg. *The Sermon on the Mount: An Exegetical Commentary*. Trans. O. C. Dean, Jr. Nashville: Abingdon Press, 1988.

Troeltsch, Ernst. "On Historical and Dogmatic Method in Theology." Pp. 729–53 in Troeltsch, *Gesammelte Schriften II. Zur religiösen Lage, Religionsphilosophie und Ethik*. Tübingen: J.C.B. Mohr/Paul Siebeck 1913.

Vermes, Geza. *The Religion of Jesus the Jew*. Minneapolis: Fortress Press, 1993.

Weiss, Johannes. *Jesus' Proclamation of the Kingdom of God*. Trans., ed., and with an introduction by Richard Hyde Hiers and David Larrimore Holland. Philadelphia: Fortress Press, 1971.

Index of Biblical Passages

Old Testament
Genesis
 14, 89
 28:10–22, 64
Exodus
 1:5, 65
 3:14, 59, 114
 8:15, 67
 18:25, 29
 20:7, 58
 20:19, 44
 23:20, 18
 24, 104–5
 33:11, 92
 33:18, 92
 33,22–23, 92
Leviticus
 11:44, 52
 19:2, 52
Numbers
 20:1–13, 87
Deuteronomy
 8:3, 25
 18:15, 13
 18:18, 92
 32:8, 65
1 Kings
 3:9, 59
 12:32, 63
 13:33, 63
2 Kings
 4:42–44, 29
Isaiah
 5:1–7, 73, 90
 6:9–10, 41, 70
 35:4, 62
 42:1, 66
 43:10–11, 115
 49:15, 58
 53:7, 19
 66:13, 58
Ezekiel
 34–37, 95
 37:15–17, 96
 37:21–22, 96
 47:1–12, 88
Hosea
 11:1–9, 76
Jonah
 1:12, 18
Zechariah
 12:10–11, 95
 13:1, 88, 96
 13:7, 95
 14:8, 88

Psalms
 2:7, 114
 22:2, 8–9
 23, 95
 23:2, 29
 31:6, 10
 44, 77
 72:4, 50
 72:12–13, 50
 73, 77
 77, 77
 77:20, 118
 91:11–12, 25
 118:22–23, 74, 90
Job
 9:8, 118
Proverbs
 8:1–21, 55
1 Chronicles
 22:9–10, 46
Sirach
 23:1, 115
 51:1, 115
 51:10, 115

New Testament
Matthew
 3:13–15, 21
 3:14–15, 20
 4:2, 24
 4:3, 24
 4:12–25, 43
 5:1–12, 49–51
 5:1–2, 54
 5:3–12, 45, 49–51
 5:3, 45
 5:5, 46, 55
 5:7, 55
 5:8, 48
 5:9, 46
 5:10, 47
 5:17–20, 49, 51
 5:17–18, 44, 48–49
 5:17, 21
 5:20, 21, 54
 5:21–7:27, 49
 5:21–48, 54
 5:23–24, 60
 6:1, 21
 6:5–8, 57
 6:9–13, 57–62
 7:12, 48
 7:28, 52, 54
 8:11–12, 29
 8:20, 45

 10:1, 64
 10:23, 106–7
 10:34, 48
 11:12, 36
 11:25–30, 55–56
 11:25–27, 114
 11:25, 52
 11:28–29, 45, 52
 12:5–8, 52
 12:18, 66
 12:28, 35, 66–67
 12:32, 66
 12:46–50, 53
 13:24–30, 36, 38–38
 16:13–20, 99
 16:16, 100
 16:21–24, 99
 16:22–23, 27
 18:12–14, 95, 97
 19:20, 52
 21:5, 55
 21:33–46, 114
 22:1–14, 114
 22:40, 48
 23:4, 55
 23:13–28, 114
 24:40–41, 42
 26:31, 95, 97
 27:46, 9
 27:55, 10
 28:18, 26, 55
 28:19, 96
Mark
 1:1, 101–2, 124 n. 4
 1:5, 18
 1:9–11, 20–22
 1:9, 21
 1.11, 102
 1:13, 23
 1:15, 35
 2:10–11, 112
 2:19, 89
 2:27–28, 111
 3:6, 41, 114
 3:11, 102
 3:13–19, 63
 4:3–8, 34, 36, 39–40
 4:10–12, 41
 4:11–12, 41, 70, 72
 4:12, 71
 4:14–20, 39–40
 4:26–29, 34, 39
 4:30–32, 34, 36
 4:35–41, 117
 5:1–20, 66

Index

5:7, 102
5:31, 29
6:34–44, 28–30
6:45–51, 116–18
7:32–37, 67
8:1–9, 29–30
8:11, 41
8:22–26, 67
8:27–30, 99
8:29, 41, 100, 102
8:31, 113–14
9:1, 104–5
9:2–8, 103–5
9:4, 102
9:7, 73, 102, 104
9:31, 113
10:18, 117
10:32–34, 113–14
10:35–40, 80
10:38, 19
11:27–33, 41
11:32, 73
12:1–12, 71–74, 90
12:9, 41, 90
13:5–37, 107
13:30, 107
14:27, 97
14:50, 97, 114
14:54, 84
14:61–62, 101
14:62, 110
15:1–20, 102
15:11–14, 73
15:34, 8–9
15:39, 20–21
15:40–41, 8, 10
Luke
1:1–4, 7–8
2:26, 100
3:7–9, 123 n. 4
3:23, 22
5:39, 65
6:20–23, 50–51
6:21, 29, 51
6:24–26, 48
8:1–3, 65
9:18–21, 99
9:20, 100
9:22–23, 99
10:1–12, 65–66
10:18, 39, 66
10:25–37, 74–75
11:1, 57
11:2–4, 57–61
11:20, 36, 66
12:50, 19
13:20–21, 34, 36
15:2, 76–77
15:4–7, 95, 97
15:8–10, 98
15:11–32, 75–77
16:19–31, 77
17:20–21, 36
17:21, 35
17:34–35, 42
23:34, 9

23:35, 100
23:42, 9
23:43, 9–10
23:46, 10
23:49, 10
24:25, 27
24:39–43, 103
24:51, 10
John
1:1, 53, 56, 103
1:18, 92, 103
1:29,19–20
1:30–33, 17
1:51, 63
2:1–12, 88–90
2:4, 91
2:17, 83
2:22, 83
3:5, 86, 88, 123 n. 5
4, 86
4:1–2, 123 n. 6
5:1–18, 86
6:1–15, 92, 94
6:16–21, 116
6:26–58, 94
6:33, 93
6:35, 93
6:51–58, 95
6:53, 93
6:63, 94
6:68–69, 100
6:69, 100
7:37–38, 87–88
7:40, 92
8:24, 115
8:28, 115
8:37–45, 114
8:46, 123 n. 5
9, 88
9:7, 86, 88
10, 96
10:1–18, 97
10:3–4, 96
10:7, 96
10:10, 96
10:14–15, 96
10:16, 96
10:17–18, 97, 113
11:16, 102
11:45–53, 77
11:49, 84
12:14–16, 83
12:24, 24, 70, 94
12:32, 71
13:4–5, 86
14:25–26, 85
15:1–10, 91
17:6, 93
18:13, 84
18:15–16, 80, 84
18:28–19:16, 83
19:25–27, 10
19:26–27, 83–84
19:30, 10
19:34–35, 80
19:34, 87–88, 96

19:35, 81
19:36, 96
20:18, 102
20:20, 102
20:24–29, 102–3
21:15–17, 96
21:22–23, 107
21:24, 80
Acts
1:1, 122 n. 8
1:8, 96
1:9, 10
1:21–22, 100
2–5, 68
7:56, 110
7:60, 9
13:32–33, 114
Romans
1:3–4, 124 n. 5
1 Corinthians
8:4–6, 64
11:26, 62
15:1–5, 37
15:5, 101
15:7, 101
15:51–52, 105
16:22, 62
2 Corinthians
5:21, 123 n. 5
Galatians
1:17–18, 125 n. 6
1:23, 17 n. 3
2:20, 22, 45
4:4, 22
Ephesians
6:10–12, 64
1 Thessalonians
2:15, 73
3:3–4, 107
4:15–17, 105–7
Hebrews
4:5, 123 n. 5
10:5–7, 125 n. 2
13:12, 77
James
1:13, 61
1 Peter
2:22, 123 n. 5
1 John
3:5: 123 n. 5
5:6–8, 87–88
Revelation
3:20, 112,
16:15, 112
22:1, 88

Gerd Lüdemann is Professor of the History and Literature of Early Christianity, Director of the Institute of Early Christian Studies, and Founder and Director of the Archive "Religionsgeschichtliche Schule" at the University of Göttingen, Germany. He is also a Visiting Scholar at Vanderbilt Divinity School in Nashville, Tennessee, a Fellow of the Jesus Seminar, and has served as co-chair of the Society of Biblical Literature Seminar on Jewish Christianity. He is the author of many books including, *The Unholy in Holy Scripture* (1997), *The Great Deception* (1999), *Paul: The Founder of Christianity* (2002), *The Resurrection of Christ* (2004), *The Acts of the Apostles* (2005), and *Intolerance and the Gospel* (2007).